ICE LEVEL

ICE LEVEL

CANADIAN HOCKEY MOMENTS FROM THE LAST 50 YEARS

✧ CANADA'S BEST FROM THE BEST ✧
EDITED AND WITH A FOREWORD BY CAM COLE

CANWEST BOOKS

Published by CanWest Books Inc.
A subsidiary of CanWest MediaWorks
1450 Don Mills Road
Toronto, ON
Canada, M3B 2X7

LIBRARY AND ARCHIVES CANADA CATALOGUING IN PUBLICATION

Ice level : Canadian hockey moments from the last 50 years : Canada's
best from the best / edited and with a foreword by Cam Cole.

ISBN 0-9736719-5-5

1. Hockey—Canada—History. I. Cole, Cam

GV848.4.C3123 2005   796.962'0971   C2005-901351-6

Pages 143 to 145 constitute a continuation of the copyright page

Jacket Design by Peter Maher/Maher Design
Text Design by Tannice Goddard/Soul Oasis Networking
Digital prepress by Emerson Group

Front Cover photographs: Peter J. Thompson/National Post (Brodeur);
Hockey Hall of Fame Archives (Richard); Wayne Cuddington/Ottawa Citizen (Crosby)
Back Cover photographs: Hockey Hall of Fame Archives (Gretzky, Orr);
Corbis Canada (Plante); Wayne Cuddington/Ottawa Citizen (Team Canada)
Printed and Bound in Canada by Friesens

First Edition

10 9 8 7 6 5 4 3 2 1

CONTENTS

FOREWORD

CAM COLE

IN LEAFING THROUGH yellowed clippings, and poring over electronic newspaper files, reading the work of the writers whose observations have shaped our view of the hockey world over the past half-century, I was struck first by the impossibility of my task.

For one thing, it is not easy finding the definitive product of the artists I considered, as an aspiring scribe, to be the icons of the trade when I was a kid in the 1950s and 60s: Jim Coleman, Milt Dunnell, Trent Frayne, Red Fisher, Scott Young, Frank Orr. That generation of larger-than-life figures put so much ribald, quirky life into painting pictures of hockey and hockey players in the days before television began giving us three dimensions and no depth.

For another, it was a conflicted assignment: were we shooting for the events, or the writing? The fact is, the memorable games, the watershed moments, were not always the best-written. That is partly a function of newspaper deadlines, and those deadlines have only gotten worse over the years at many papers. On game night, today's ink-stained wretch is required to pound out hurried, stream-of-consciousness stories with not enough time to craft them into poetry — which is how the earlier writers' work used to sound, to my ears.

So some of the most moving pieces I encountered, especially of recent vintage, were about personalities, and only peripherally about the games.

Furthermore, though a good deal of the country's best hockey writing appeared in the pages of newspapers belonging to what is now CanWest MediaWorks — the Southam chain of papers, in a former life — we didn't have a monopoly on it, by any means. And some of the papers that contained original work we would love to have seen are no more.

And so, where we needed to fill obvious gaps, we appealed to the libraries of the Toronto Star, The Globe and Mail, and Sun Media, and the works of their terrific writers were generously provided.

But our database was, first and foremost, the product of our own craftsmen who worked for CanWest — and that is a stable which has included some of the finest writers of hockey who ever typed for a living: among them, Roy MacGregor, who probably understands hockey's place in the Canadian consciousness better than anyone, Michael Farber, who left the Montreal Gazette in 1994 to fight the good fight on behalf of our game in the pages of Sports Illustrated (more's the pity), the irrepressible Coleman, a giant of the industry, and Jim Taylor, who turned a witty phrase as effortlessly as Wayne Gretzky flipped a saucer-pass.

You will notice some imbalances, partly due to the difficulties of micro-filmed or paper archives, which led to there being far more material from the 1970s onward than from the 1960s back.

In a few cases, where writers' work is preserved in anthologies, we were able to find gems such as the ageless Toronto Star columnist Milt Dunnell's wonderful take on the overtime goal Leafs defenceman Bobby Baun scored on a frozen ankle in the 1964 Stanley Cup final.

Other times, we were lucky enough to have gems fall from the heavens. After Coleman's death in 2000, Taylor discovered fourteen boxes full of the master's old columns, dating from 1939, which by rights ought to be declared national treasures. Taylor passed a couple of them on for this collection — including Coleman's rollicking account of the deciding game of the 1972 Canada-Soviet summit series (which I have paired with a clever, bigger-picture column by Taylor himself, filed the same night.)

For some momentous evenings, we found rich memories contained in a series Fisher produced for the Montreal Gazette in the fall of 2004, when the

NHL season that would have been his 50th was put on hold by the NHL's labour dispute. Fisher's series gave us first-person accounts of the Rocket Richard Riot in 1955, the night goalie Jacques Plante donned the mask for the first time in a game, and the 1975 New Year's Eve game between the Canadiens and the Soviet Red Army.

We note the dates of publication of the stories, but for purposes of this book, they are arranged chronologically by the time to which they refer — either to an era or to a specific date — from the tale of the men who won Olympic hockey gold for Canada in 1952 to the present day.

The stories in this anthology include everything from a pair of beautifully written offerings on the vigil for an icon and the mortality of aging Olympians by Christie Blatchford ... to a straight obituary on one of hockey's great characters, Badger Bob Johnson, rendered eloquently by Eric Duhatschek in the Calgary Herald, with a last line that will make you cry (no peeking) ... to an essay on the simple things by MacGregor that doesn't seem to be about one of hockey's greatest moments, but which could stand as a lament on the hockey lockout of 2004-05. It was written ten years earlier.

Time has been remarkably kind to the stories reprinted here, but you may get a chuckle now and then from old-time expressions, and dollar figures that evidently seemed outrageous in their day, and seem absurdly tiny today. There are fearless predictions that didn't come true, and others that did, but such is life for sportswriters.

The problem of uneven access led to an editing challenge: how to balance the content so that the 1950s don't appear to be entirely about Richard, and the 1980s onward don't all appear to be about Gretzky. And yet, those two athletes run like a river through the story of hockey in the latter half of the 20th century and the first few years of this one. To deny their proper place is to ignore two major influences on what it is that we love about the game. If they seem to take up an inordinate amount of space in this collection, the fault is my own.

Finally, a word to young readers about the World Hockey Association, which appears in several stories in this collection — stories about Gretzky and Mark Messier, who began their careers in the rebel league, and Bobby Hull and Gordie Howe, who signed to play in the WHA as older stars. Formed in 1972 and gone by 1979, when four of its teams were absorbed into the NHL (which was eager to end the salary escalation caused by having to bid for players' services), the WHA had an enduring influence on the professional game, on players' compensation, and on the NHL's view of expansion in general. It was also, for those who experienced its cheeky irreverence, pure fun to cover.

At best, a book like this is a series of snapshots, each meant to convey a feeling or a moment, and it is, by definition, entirely subjective. A thousand great moments didn't find their way into these pages. It occurs to me that I have used too many pieces by particular favourites — in some cases, because they happened to be where the action was; now and then because the subject matter touched me the first time I read them. I have also omitted altogether some very fine work by writers I admire immensely. To them, I apologize.

Enough terrific hockey stories made the short-list to fill two or three books like this one. Alas, as with my own daily columns in the Vancouver Sun, National Post, and the CanWest chain, the publisher told me my short-list needed editing.

The winter of 2004-05 was a long, dark one for hockey fans, many of whom don't care how much their favorite players earn or whether an owner is turning a handsome profit on his investment, but only want to be carried away by the moment, as hockey at it best does so splendidly.

The stories in this book are, by and large, about memorable people and unforgettable games. With the passage of time, the dollars seem remarkably unimportant.

Cam Cole
July 27, 2005

MERCURYS PASS THE GREAT TORCH

CHRISTIE BLATCHFORD

February 25, 2002 — *National Post*

SALT LAKE CITY — In the stands at the Team Canada end of the rink yesterday, sitting in pairs, the four old men watched as their time finally, irrevocably, passed before their watery eyes.

They are among 12 surviving players from the 1952 Olympic champion Edmonton Mercurys.

They could not have been happier or more graceful, and that is why hockey is great, because it breeds this goodness in men.

Every time the young Canadians scored, 75-year-old Donnie Gauf, the one nicknamed Choo-Choo, would jump to his feet, give a two-thumbs signal, and clap his still-immense farmer's hands. Eric Paterson, the man beside him, at 69 thin and with the sort of lovely freckled transparency that aging skin sometimes acquires, would rise, too, but in the watchful way that Martin Brodeur would recognize in a minute: Once a goalie, always a goalie.

Higher up, in the last row of Section 107, were the two Billys.

In the aisle seat was Gibby, his beautiful broad face breaking into periodic grins.

Next to him was The Senator, and it is easy to see why he had that name because he has the *gravitas* of the natural captain — and because he was still looking after his boys, even now. Bill Gibson, 74, is weak from his radiation

5

treatments and had stumbled alarmingly on the steep stairs at the E Center a few days before, and Bill Dawe, three years his senior, was toning down his own still vigorous instincts to get to his feet in a gesture of love for his friend.

They were brought to Salt Lake and given their last hurrah by Labatt's, the big brewery: How perfect is that?

Fifty years before, the Mercs were playing the Yanks for gold at the Jordal Amphia, an outdoor arena, in Oslo, Norway. Choo-Choo scored to put the Canucks ahead 3-2, but the Americans tied it, and the Mercs won the gold on the point system that was used in those days, when it was an eight-game tournament, every win worth two points.

The Mercs paid for their rooms at the Olympic Village — university dormitories — by playing an extra game on the pre-Games tour that took them all over Europe and gave the 16 players, one coach and a trainer a glamorous taste of postwar Europe in an era when air travel was the preserve of the rich. Some of them, this trip rendered sophisticates with a taste for travel; The Senator went overseas again a couple of times with his wife. Choo-Choo never got bit by that bug; he returned from Oslo with an engagement ring for the woman who would become his bridge-playing wife, Joan.

The Mercurys were amateurs. Most of them worked for Jim Christiansen, who owned the big Waterloo Mercury Lincoln dealership in Edmonton. Choo-Choo, was the new truck manager and The Senator was the parts manager. Others were firemen. Everyone had a real job. Everyone also had a family to feed or bills to pay, so when they headed off, qualifying as the Canadian Olympic entrant by winning the *Edmonton Journal* Trophy and the western championship, Mr. Christiansen called every single man in for a chat, and made sure every man's family was paid while the team was gone for almost four months.

"He probably spent $100,000 out of his own pocket," The Senator said the other day. The Mercs revere Mr. Christiansen still, and have gone to bat to get his name included with theirs in the Hockey Hall of Fame.

He went with them on the tour, but he fell sick in Europe, gritted it out to see them win, and came back to an Edmonton hospital bed he never left.

"We're better people for knowing him," said Choo-Choo.

There were no helmets then, no face masks for Mr. Paterson and the other goalies. Their sticks were wood, their pads of soft leather. They got two pairs each of Tackaberry skates, and their uniforms. No fans travelled with them and the only media came from newspaper writers and radio guys. All their games were played outdoors because Olympic rules didn't allow a roof over the ice.

The team was based in London, and would fly out to Sweden or Italy for their pre-Olympic games.

In Milan, they remember, their thoughtful hosts served them after-dinner drinks "and all the wrong things" as The Senator said, between periods. In Zurich, they stayed at a glorious hotel called the Doldrum, and when they were reluctantly leaving, the hotel manager came running out after the bus, and held it until he had the players all open their luggage: Out came 16 of the posh bath towels the prairie boys had never seen the likes of before.

In London, they stayed at the Rose Court Hotel, and when The Senator went back to England years later, he and his wife went there and found it is now a nursing home.

They are not so far from needing a place like that themselves. As Choo-Choo said, with a cheerful remarkable bluntness, "I came because this might be the last time." His listener asked if he meant that because the next Winter Games are in Turin, Italy, the Mercs wouldn't make the trip? "No," he said, "I mean, because it might be the last one for us."

They have had a blast in Salt Lake, rooms at the best joint in town, the Hotel Monaco, and soirées at Canada Lodge, tickets to the games worth $425 a pop.

One day, in the Canadian dressing room at the E Center, Choo-Choo found Mario Lemieux being worked on for a charley horse in his right leg and threw him in a headlock. The Senator had a very quiet word with Stevie Yzerman and was there when his wife returned from the Roots store, loaded down with parcels, and Mr. Yzerman groaned at the sight. He asked Mr. Yzerman how the players ranked the Olympic gold. "He said it's unbelievable, the priority we put on it," The Senator said. "He said the National Hockey League games are kind of blah, they play so many." They talked to Kevin Lowe, one of Wayne Gretzky's assistants. They saw Ryan Smyth with a cut from a slash over his eye, and it was Billy Gibson, I think, who said, "What girl hit you?"

All the Team Canada players laughed at that, Choo-Choo said.

The four Mercs saw their team picture in the dressing room, too.

When the young Canadians won yesterday, I was watching the Mercs through my binoculars.

As, on the ice, the players fell on Mr. Brodeur, and wept with relief and joy, and wives came down to the boards to blow kisses and weep — Joe Nieuwendyk's little girl, Tyra, being passed from one hand to another until she finally was taken by her daddy — the four old men stood and stared.

They saw Mr. Gretzky wait a full five minutes before emerging on the bench; they love Wayne. They would not have been surprised that he knew to let the players have their time alone. They saw these big men, the most immense monkey in the world off their backs, caress and hug with such tenderness. They saw them cheer the Americans, and celebrate with the shy decency of Canadian hockey players.

Even before the anthem played and the flag rose high, Choo-Choo took off his red hat.

When *O Canada* was over, I looked for them, but they had gone. They had a half-century of glory and wonder, but there was not a shred of regret that it was over. They had passed the great Canadian torch to safe hands. It was time to go home.

LIGHTING THE FLAME OF REVOLUTION

RED FISHER

September 26, 2004 — *The Gazette (Montreal)*

ALMOST 36 YEARS after he had played his last game with the Canadiens, Maurice Richard stood on the Montreal Forum ice with tears streaming down his face as the noise grew and grew ... minute after minute until there was no longer merely noise in this hockey cathedral, but an outpouring of love engulfing it. Now and then, he would raise his arms pleading to the people.

"Enough," he seemed to be saying to them on this March 11, 1996, evening, the night the building's lights would go dark forever for hockey. "Enough! I was only a hockey player."

There are memorable games and there are people in it who will never be forgotten — none more so than The Rocket, who in 1945 became the first NHL player to score 50 goals in a 50-game season. His 544 goals in 978 regular-season games still stands as an all-time high for the Canadiens.

He was the most intense athlete this game, this city, this province, this country ever has seen. He was everything that personified greatness. It was in this place that he was to become an icon, a legend. He was one of a kind.

His best years already were behind him when I started covering the Canadiens at the start of the 1955-56 season. By then, after 13 NHL seasons, he had lost a step. But now and then in his last five seasons, he was once again The Rocket, and on those nights, there was no finer sight anywhere.

In July 1975, almost 15 years after Richard's retirement, playwright Rick Salutin sat with me outside Banff, Alberta. He had been commissioned to write a play about Les Canadiens.

"Tell me about the Canadiens," he said. "What do they mean to the people of Quebec?"

I told Salutin that if you fight but don't win the real battle against those who are perceived to be the rulers, you try to win elsewhere in a forum where you are successful. In other words, on the ice with the Canadiens. Later, in an introduction to his play, which was first performed in Montreal in February 1977, he wrote that it was very much the same answer he got at a bar in Quebec City.

"I watched a hockey game on television and marvelled at the frenzied involvement of the patrons," he wrote. "I put to my drinking partner this question: 'How come?'

"She said: 'The Canadiens — they're us. Every winter they go south and in the spring they come home conquerors.'"

Richard was their commander-in-chief, and if he had been "only a hockey player," his suspension for the final week of the 1954-55 regular season and the playoffs after getting involved in a savage, stick-swinging duel with Boston defenceman Hal Laycoe would have been little more than a hiccup in NHL history. Instead, it fanned the flames of a cultural revolution that went far, far beyond Richard, the player.

Has it really been almost five decades since that St. Patrick's Day in 1955? The memory lingers and always shall, but where have the years flown? There was a hint of snow in the air, but nobody in Montreal was thinking about the weather on this day. The Detroit Red Wings were in the city, but the Canadiens would be playing without Richard. His people were in a foul mood. There was trouble ahead. You could sense it ... breathe in the ugly, sour smell of it.

The dangerous stick-swinging fracas which led to Richard's suspension had happened the previous Sunday. It erupted when the generally mild-mannered Laycoe had struck Richard on the side of the head with his stick. Richard responded by high-sticking Laycoe on the shoulder and face. Then, when Richard's stick was taken from him, he grabbed another and struck Laycoe twice on the back.

The day before this Canadiens-Red Wings game, NHL president Clarence Campbell brought down the decision that shook the hockey establishment in general and Canadiens fans in particular. Richard, poised to win his first-ever scoring title, was suspended for the remaining three games of the regular season. He was also suspended for the playoffs. Gone was his opportunity to win the scoring title. Also apparently gone were the Canadiens' hopes in the playoffs.

President Campbell rarely missed a game at the Forum, and despite being urged by Montreal mayor Jean Drapeau not to attend the game, Campbell arrived at his Forum seat about 15 rows above ice level halfway through the first period. Not surprisingly, his arrival attracted angry cries and loud, boisterous threats from groups of fans. Eggs and tomatoes were thrown, but the worst was yet to come.

At period's end, with the Red Wings leading 4-1, a fan approached Campbell, his hand outstretched to the president. Then, when Campbell reached for his hand, he was slapped in the face. Seconds later, a tear-gas bomb exploded, sending terrified fans streaming toward the Forum exits. People were coughing and retching, their eyes streaming. Many yelled "fire." The building was ordered cleared and game was forfeited to the visitors.

Outside the building, a crowd of several thousand people gathered and in a matter minutes, an angry mob of hooligans started marching along the city's main street, shattering windows, looting and burning along the way. Thirty-seven adults and four juveniles were arrested. The wonder of it, though, was that nobody was killed on that black night which has become known as the Richard Riot.

What is it about an athlete who could inflame his people this way?

Others could skate faster than Richard. Some could shoot harder and pass better. Nobody, however, approached his intensity from the blue line in. Nobody wanted to win more. Not Gordie Howe. Not Wayne Gretzky. Not Mario Lemieux. Not anybody.

He brought the entire package to the arena. He ignited a fire under his people on and off the ice. He stirred their souls like no other player before him or since.

He was, after all, The Rocket.

THE MAN
IN THE MASK

RED FISHER

September 24, 2004 — *The Gazette (Montreal)*

THE LATE JACQUES Plante always will be remembered among the truly great goaltenders for an amalgam of reasons. It's there in his numbers: five consecutive Stanley Cups with the Canadiens dynasty from 1955-56 through the 1959-60 season; winner of the Vezina Trophy in each of those seasons, seven in all, and the Hart Trophy in 1962.

Was he the best goaltender of all time ahead of, let's say, Terry Sawchuk? It's something that has been debated for decades, but there's no argument that he was the greatest innovator of all time, starting with the night of Nov. 1, 1959.

The Canadiens were in New York to face the Rangers, and a little more than three minutes into the game, Andy Bathgate moved in on Plante and delivered a short backhander that struck the goaltender in the face, opening a savage cut that started at the corner of his mouth and ran in an ugly red line through a nostril.

Plante sprawled on his stomach, his head cushioned in a pool of blood. (Years later, Bathgate admitted the move had been premediated, because seconds earlier the goaltender had chased the Rangers superstar into the corner for a loose puck.) Helping hands guided Plante into the medical room, where he shook off the supporting arms.

He moved in front of the mirror.

"Before you do anything, I want to see what it looks like," he told the doctor.

Later, bits of loose flesh were scraped away from the wound, and as Plante lay there, his fingers interlocked, the doctor's needle knifed through the raw flesh.

Twenty minutes later, Plante left the room and skated to the Canadiens' room to the lively rendition of *For He's a Jolly Good Fellow* from the Madison Square Garden organist.

"How bad is it?" coach Toe Blake asked.

"It's sore," Plante said.

It wasn't until years later that the two-goalie system was adopted, so Blake had this suggestion: "Why don't you wear your mask for the rest of the game?"

If Blake hadn't suggested it, Plante would have. For some weeks, he had been thinking about wearing a mask, arguing that curved blades had started to appear, players were shooting harder, so was it really necessary for goaltenders to stand there while pucks came at them through forests of players? He had spent a lot of time with equipment manufacturers promoting the idea. OK, so maybe it would be more difficult to see a puck at his feet, but wasn't that better than no mask at all?

"I don't think I can go back in without it," Plante told Blake.

Bathgate's mean-spirited backhander had been the Rangers' third shot, and Plante somehow allowed only one goal on the 25 shots he was to face the rest of the game. The Canadiens won and, as you'd expect, the game result was hardly mentioned in the post-game media scrum. What about the mask? Could he see properly with it? Did he feel more confident with it?

Plante sat there, fresh blood dribbling from below the patch that covered his wound. Another patch, caked with dried blood, covered a five-stitch cut on his chin he had suffered a week earlier in a game against Chicago.

"What bothered me most of all was that I swallowed some blood," Plante told reporters. "I didn't feel too bad and my teeth felt numb. I wouldn't have played without it."

Then he paused and added: "Well ... maybe I would have."

Coach Blake had other ideas. "He can practise with one, if he wants," he said, "but no goaltender of mine is gonna wear one in a game. We're here to win!"

Plante didn't wear the mask in the next game, but insisted on wearing it in the game after that and, once he did, the game for goaltenders was changed forever.

Plante was different. He wasn't intimidated easily. He had firm ideas about what was good for the game and for him. He would do what he felt was right for him — on and off the ice. What was good for him, he insisted, was right for the Canadiens and for hockey.

The truth is, Blake loved Plante, the goaltender, but didn't like him as a person. The Canadiens didn't like surprises, and Plante was full of them. On some nights, Blake would arrive at the arena and find Plante waiting for him.

"I don't think I can play tonight," he would say.

"What's the problem?"

"My asthma," Plante said.

Later, Blake would fume. "That sob is driving me nuts. I never can be sure when he's playing, but he always ends up playing. I don't know how much more of this I can take."

Know something? While Blake at times hated Plante, he always insisted he was the best goaltender he'd ever seen.

"Especially those five years we won the Cup, eh?" Blake said. "I played with (Bill) Durnan, and he was the best I'd ever seen up to that time. Plante was better during those five years."

Blake knew it and so did Plante. His teammates knew it, even though he stretched their patience from time to time. It's true he played behind many of hockey's best players, starting with Doug Harvey on defence, Jean Béliveau, Dickie Moore, Maurice and Henri Richard, Boom-Boom Geoffrion and others. The result was that on some nights, Plante's work was minimal because his colleagues controlled the puck most of the game, but he always made the big stops when the Canadiens needed them. No goaltender I have ever known was more confident in his ability to win.

Harvey won his sixth Norris Trophy as the NHL's best defenceman during the 1960-61 season, yet despite his dominance at the position he was traded to the New York Rangers for Lou Fontinato.

"How much is this team going to miss Doug?" I asked Plante on the first day of training camp.

"I figured that would be the first question I'd be asked in training camp," Plante replied with a grin. "Listen: Doug Harvey is the greatest defenceman in the National Hockey League. All of us — Jean, Dickie, Boom Boom, Henri — especially me, we owe him a lot. He helped me win five Vezinas in a row, but now, I'm going to show everybody how good Jacques Plante is. I'm going to win the Vezina without him."

"You're kidding, right?"

"Watch me!"

The Canadiens allowed only 166 goals that season, 22 fewer than the previous year. They finished in first place with 98 points, 13 ahead of the second-place Toronto Maple Leafs. Plante played 70 games and won his sixth Vezina.

The Man in the Mask also won the Hart as the NHL's most valuable player. Rangers defenceman Doug Harvey finished second in the voting.

LONG LIVE THE KING
AND LEAFS THE NAME

JACK KINSELLA

April 23, 1962 — *The Ottawa Citizen*

CHICAGO — In the aftermath of victory, the delirious dressing room of the new world champions was a reasonable facsimile of the Black Hole of Calcutta. The difference was that in this dungeon everyone was sopping up champagne like it was going out of style.

Among the happy Leafs, there was contrasting reaction in the middle of the tumult. The younger players lived it up excitedly, savouring the first taste of Stanley Cup wine. Along the walls, the veterans merely slumped, happy but still exhausted. Later, perhaps, but not now.

Wending his way slowly around the room through the milling mob and deafening clamour, coach Punch Imlach shook hands with each of his players and said a few unheard words in each ear.

"We can let it out now," said Imlach over the bedlam. "Pulford played with a shoulder frozen and Stewart had his rib frozen. I think the whole team played a great game and did it the hard way.

"But the greatest thing," he said proudly, "was that we did it right here on Chicago ice. They'll never be able to say we were homers."

If the Black Hawks had managed to pull out a victory in this one, in the interests of justice they would have had to arrest someone. Rudy Pilous' team was never in the game, their brief third-period lead notwithstanding.

"Aw, let's face it," muttered Bobby Hull in the gloomy Hawks' barracks at the other end of the Chicago Stadium. "They not only outchecked us, but outplayed us as well. We just didn't have it."

It was obvious almost from the opening whistle and I suspect that even the crowd sensed impending disaster. It was the quietest crowd I've ever heard in the Stadium. Only when Bobby Hull gave the Hawks a brief lead, did they come to life with any of their old authority and noise, and with something new in Chicago — a barrage of old hats.

"Listen," growled Pilous. "if we couldn't protect that goal with about 11 minutes to play, we didn't deserve to win. That penalty (to Eric Nesterenko which opened the way for the winning goal) really hurt us but that should be no excuse."

If it was a happy evening for the Leafs, however, it was something special for the hero of the game. For a while it looked as if Richard Duff was due for a horn fitting. It was Duff who inadvertently shoved the puck out from behind the Toronto net onto Bobby Hull's stick, and almost gave the Hawks the shot in the arm they needed to commit grand larceny.

But, less than seven minutes later, Duff came back to redeem himself when he fired home what proved to be the big one. It took everyone by surprise, including Duff.

"I picked up Army's (George Armstrong's) pass behind me, whirled, and shot," he said, "but I didn't know it went in. Glenn Hall had gone down to block and I couldn't see. But wow, what a thrill when that light went on."

Almost as important a goal, however, was Bob Nevin's tying marker because it was the first time the Leafs had been able to dent the armour of Hall, even though they'd had enough chances to win a dozen games. If he'd missed from that range, they might never have found the Leafian Leader in time for the seventh game.

In the Leaf dressing room, everyone was firing questions at the Leader about the future.

"I don't want to think about anything," parried Imlach with a tired smile. "But I will say this, if my bosses are happy with me, I'd like to be back with these guys in the same capacity."

It must be the understatement of the series. If the Silver Seven isn't happy with the man who brought them their first Stanley Cup in 11 years, they'd be liable to tarring and feathering by the fans.

This team was full value for their victory and a lot of the credit has to go to Imlach. He started almost from scratch, mixing extreme youth with a judicious supply of supposedly castoff veterans. It took four years, but it was a successful formula.

Somehow, though, the Leafs themselves must have suspected it would be their night. Several of the players were hardly in the dressing room before they had unlimbered their own flash cameras to take photographs.

This Leaf team, it seems to me, may be taking more photographs in the next few years.

The king is dead, long live the king — and the name is Toronto Maple Leafs.

BEST SHOT CAME FROM A NEEDLE

MILT DUNNELL

April 24, 1964 — *The Toronto Star*

DETROIT — The pen, of course, is mightier than the sword. So is the needle.

After the Torontos and the Detroits had duelled to the verge of complete exhaustion last night, it took a few cc's of a local anaesthetic to turn the tide of battle in favour of the sweaty horde from Hogtown on the Humber.

The name of the magic fluid shall remain unmentioned — for fear somebody tries it on a racehorse and it shows up in the saliva test. In that event, the stewards would hold up the purse and suspend the trainer.

Injected into Bobby Baun's ankle, the stuff practically changed the course of history. Instead of being the first big-league shinny club in 15 years to get rubbed out by a fourth-place team in the final scramble for Lord Stanley's tinware, the Leafs could be the first since the invention of the puck to win the old cuspidor for three-year spans in two different eras.

Maybe that sounds like being the first left-handed Eskimo to get his right hand frozen twice on Baffin Island. However, it is much better than getting kicked in the face with a stiff boot — and that's what was happening to the Leafs when the needle was jabbed into Baun's ankle.

Things started getting rough for our heroes about 15:06 of the second period. It was at that point that Gordie Howe dumped the puck into the Leaf net while our Mr. Tim Horton lay flat on his back just inside the Leaf blue line. This was a greater outbreak of intrigue than the uprising in Zanzibar. Parker McDonald of the Wings rapped Horton briskly with his stick behind the knees as he moved over to meet the challenge from Howe. Tim went down like a keg of nails falling off a hardware truck.

With the whole right side of the Toronto defence thus torn open, Howe had no trouble scoring the goal which gave the Wings a 3-2 margin. Horton appealed in vain for justice to prevail — but justice was blind.

"While I was in the air, I looked over and saw that [referee Vern] Buffey was watching," Horton related later. "Naturally, I expected a penalty on the play. I can fall on my rump often enough without getting help from Parker McDonald."

Billy Harris, revelling in his parole from custody on the end of the Leaf bench, tied the score again at 17:48 of the period. When the teams left the ice for a siesta, the Leafs were in a most favourable position. Albert Langlois of the Wings still had one minute and 45 seconds to serve in a penalty.

But strange are the moods and fatigues that affect athletes. When the warriors returned to the ice, you had to look twice to see whether the Leafs had brought their skates with them. They were dying in their tracks. Aside from Bob Pulford, Baun and possibly one or two others, the seats of their pantaloons were dragging.

When Baun was hauled off on a stretcher at 13:14, the only thing that remained to be decided was whether services for the Leafs should be public or private. Word reached the press box that Baun's right ankle was sprained or broken. In five minutes, he was back.

This led to a rumour that Jim Murray, the Leaf doctor, had hacked a leg off Eddie Shack and changed Baun's flat tire. As it turned out, Baun's ankle had merely been frozen. It's just possible the puck was given an injection, too. When Baun fired it from the Detroit blue line, after only one minute and 43 seconds of overtime, the old biscuit did some strange things.

One witness was Mr. William Gadsby, who is described as an old resident. Mr. Gadsby said the thing was spinning like a drunk in a revolving door. As it neared him, Mr. Gadsby said, the infernal thing dived at him. He fled, but it skipped off the handle of his shillelagh. Next thing he knew, it had hopped past Terry Sawchuk and was high in the net. Mr. Sawchuk was interviewed, too — but everything he said was unprintable.

This will become known to posterity as the drugstore goal. Now, if the Leafs can just transplant a new ankle on Baun before Saturday night, they may be guests at a champagne party. Now that his own ankle has thawed out, it probably won't be good enough.

THE WORD IS DEFIANCE

DICK BEDDOES

May 3, 1967 — *The Globe and Mail*

THERE HAD BEEN heavy rain in the afternoon, and in the early evening, the reflections of street lamps lay in trifling pools on Carlton Street.

People moved quickly down the street, funnelled toward the Gardens, all of them hurried by an urgency they shared. Win or lose, the sixth game of the Stanley Cup final was the last hockey game the Leafs would play in Toronto this spring. It was the last game some of them would play in Toronto, period.

At least one guy who tries as a rule to observe sport dispassionately had the forlorn feeling that comes from the inevitable, "So long and see ya." Evening has caught some of the Leafs, too, but it is a shiny darkness, brightened by the reflections of other years. When they skated out against the Canadiens, it was the last time you will see them as they were, on good nights this season.

Some will retire, and some will depart in the expansion draft, and when they won the Cup last night, it was an unexpected prize. They made the playoffs as almost everybody expected (except this department, which picked 'em fifth!), then advanced to the final round, as almost nobody thought possible. They kept coming back with a defiance that makes you appreciate what they are, and before the sixth game Tim Horton talked about that. He talked about it with casual maturity, amused by the brittle

22

praise that accompanies winning. "You know what they say," Horton was saying, "Goalkeeping is like pitching." He gazed across the dressing room, into the corner where Terry Sawchuk was strapping on the bulky tools of his trade. "If Sawchuk is Koufax tonight, we win. If he isn't ..." — a shrug punctuated the simplicity of his explanation — "well, as they say in Montreal, *c'est la guerre.*"

It is war, all right — Sandy Koufax overpowering enemy batsmen when he was right, making the Dodgers better than they were; or Sawchuk, in these playoffs, challenging the big shooters to drive the puck past him, giving the Leafs the security that comes with shutout pitching.

Bob Baun stood beside Horton, shoulder harness dragged over his head and arms, pausing to add what he feels about the goalkeeper.

"Getting up for a game has got to be a lot mental with Ukey," mentioning Sawchuk with the nickname he is rarely called beyond the dressing room. "Watch him in practice or pre-game warmups, it doesn't tear him up if he gets beaten. He'll kind of nonchalant the puck, except once or twice. But once or twice in the warmup, you'll see Ukey get the feel. He'll charge out to cut down the angle a shooter has to score." There was a touch of professional admiration in Baun's voice. "When Ukey charges out, all you see to shoot at is a damn big goalie."

Sawchuk has not retreated from earlier hints that he wants to return to Detroit, either to retire and join his father-in-law in a golf course business or to finish his career where it began. He has earned the privilege, at 37, of finally calling the shots on himself. But chances are, if he cares to keep playing, George Imlach will want a warm body or two from the Red Wings in exchange.

Now it was war, and Sawchuk was the way Conn Smythe was to describe the game afterward — "the leader of a bunch of game guys who went over the top in 1917!"

He was commanding, outstanding, and also pretty good. Goals the Canadiens scored in a taut first period weren't goals because Sawchuk got there first, shutting off the daylight the shots were aimed at. In civilian life, he would have received a 10-year rap for larceny.

The Canadiens kept coming at him, but it was testimony to the Leafs' relentless checking that the losers never had a good scoring chance in the

14 minutes after Dick Duff scored their first goal.

Finally, George Armstrong let the last ounce of pressure out of the boiler with 43 seconds left — a goal into an empty Montreal net — and Sawchuk's ordeal was over. He seemed to sag, as though this was Koufax and his last pitch had subdued the last batter in the World Series.

Then tumult piled on turmoil with every exuberant in the diocese loose, clambering down to the Leafs' bench. You could have run a fish net from Carlton Street to Hamilton and not caught a single inferiority complex.

Sawchuk escaped to the dressing room, not waiting for Clarence Campbell's presentation of the Stanley Cup to Armstrong, finished after a long season he almost didn't begin. He sat for a long time, head down, big hands cupped around a Coke, trying to absorb what had happened to him.

He looked up after several silent minutes, eyes bloodshot, the sweat coming off him. "My greatest thrill," he murmured. "Absolutely, the greatest."

Comment came out of him heavily, the way it does when fatigue catches up and removes, even for victors, the jubilation. "I almost went home from training camp," he admitted. "The back operation still bothered me, and I was discouraged."

But his spine improved and he survived and when Johnny Bower was knocked out of the playoffs before the first game, Sawchuk came in from the bullpen. Now wet underwear hung on his gaunt frame, and he took the occasional sustenance from a cigarette.

Sawchuk was disciplined during the game, making the moves of the most stylish goaler extant, allowing the frustrated Canadiens scarcely a single rebound. "Discipline is hardly the word," he said, smiling small. "I was scared every time they got near me. Scared witless."

The last trace of getting up for a major travail was gone, the last emotion wrung out of him. "I wouldn't want to play another game," he said, more to himself than to succeeding hordes of celebrating fans. "Not one."

Statisticians can't use their arithmetic to measure Sawchuk and Kelly and Stanley and Horton and Pronovost and Pulford and Keon and the rest in these playoffs. They had loyalty to a hope that few outside the dressing room believed existed. Sawchuk certified that hope, and last night may be the last time he passed this way as a Leaf.

We'll be talking about him a long time after he's gone.

BENNY AND THE JET

JIM TAYLOR

June 28, 1972 — *The Vancouver Sun*

WINNIPEG — For hitting a piece of rubber with a stick, Bobby Hull now makes far more money than president, prime minister, or Jonas Salk the year he beat polio.

Yesterday, in St. Paul, Minnesota, they handed him a cheque for $1 million. Three hours later, he was in Winnipeg, signing for another $2 million. We live in a brave new sports era, the day of the Instant Millionaire. You can't help but wonder if this was how it was in Rome just before the Huns came over the wall.

Say $3 million, and the mind buckles after the third zero. I touched the cheques and will never wash again. To get an idea of how it was on the World Hockey Association bread-and-circuses route Tuesday, consider this: If a man born today lived his allotted three score and ten, to pay him $3 million you'd have to give him $117.42 every day of his life. Think about that when you drive your kid to the orthodontist.

For Hull, the $3 million is merely a beginning. Endorsements will be available as fast as he can sign his name. And if there's one thing Bobby can do, it's sign his name.

He's been signing it for 14 years. More than any other NHL player, he has always been available for autograph hounds, standing with inexhaustible patience signing over and over again: BEST WISHES, BOBBY HULL. BEST WISHES,

BOBBY HULL. The words are so deeply burned in his brain, it's said, that when he says his prayers he signs off: BEST WISHES, BOBBY HULL.

He was signing again yesterday, proving Gentle Ben Hatskin was right. It took him half-an-hour to wade through the 5,000 people between his car and the hotel where they held the second signing. "How in blazes," Hatskin said wonderingly, "did Chicago ever let that one get away?"

The Hull charisma, as the Hull slap shot, convinced Benny that he was worth the $3 million it took to bring him to the Winnipeg Jets. "It's a gamble, sure," he admitted Monday. "But not as much as people think."

Hatskin was sitting in his office in his big, black chair, apologizing because the coffee perc didn't work and he didn't know whether he could afford to get it fixed. As he talked, he gummed home-rolled cigarettes. ("You can save a lot with these, you know. Thirty-four cents a pack compared to 60. It adds up.")

Hatskin also had plans for Hull. "When he gets here, I'm gonna take him to centre ice and point up to a section where there's about 1,000 seats. 'Those are your responsibility, baby,' I'll say. 'There damn well better be behinds in them.'"

But shed no tears for Benny. His $2 million is safe. He could even be turning a profit by year end.

The delicious part of it all is that, just when the WHA deal with Hull seemed ready to fall apart, the NHL stepped in and saved it.

Some WHA owners were reluctant to part with their share of the Hull bonus. For a few hours it was dicey. Then the NHL bypassed Cleveland and gave a franchise to Washington, which so angered Cleveland's Nick Mileti that he jumped to the WHA, handing over $250,000 for the idle Calgary franchise. The money reduced everybody's share of the Hull deal to $68,000, and although some of them still haven't paid, it made the difference between getting Hull and losing him. "I must write Clarence Campbell and say thank you," muses Gentle Ben.

In St. Paul, the WHA people crowed and the Bobby Hull Joke was born. For his ranch, he'd chosen Saskatchewan. The new Bobby Hull table hockey game will be just like the old one, only the players will move slower.

Dennis Murphy, co-founder of the WHA, ran around telling people about the new owner in Ottawa. "We've got 12 solid franchises now — 12!" he yelled. "Next year, Europe!"

Good grief — three million rubles for Anatoli Firsov.

Waiting in the airport, his $1-million cheque tucked safely away, Hull headed for the pay phones.

"Hey, Bobby!" yelled Benny the Hat. "You got change?"

NEVER
A DOUBT

JIM COLEMAN

September 29, 1972 — *Southam News*

MOSCOW — I don't know what the heck you were worrying about. I kept telling you that Canada would make a clean sweep of this series on Moscow ice. I can hardly wait to get home to have a few words with those wisenheimers who have been sending me all that charming mail.

Mind you, there were a few occasions yesterday when the confidence of even the most loyal Canadian wavered. At the end of the second period, when the Soviets were leading 5-3, things looked so bleak that a couple of us went up to the press bar on the fourth floor of the Moscow Sports Palace and ordered some of those salami sandwiches that they import from Minsk. They only import the bread from Minsk — the salami runs wild around here.

We were washing down the salami with a stout drencher of chloride of lime when a courier dashed in with the news that Phil Esposito had reduced the margin to 5-4 on a pass from Pete Mahovlich.

"Order me a double vodka," said my Canadian companion, "this is the only place to get a really dispassionate view of the game."

He was just downing the double vodka when the courier rushed back with the further intelligence that Rodrique (Mad Dog) Gilbert, the comely right-winger, had scored a clean-cut fistic decision over Evgeni Mishakov at 3:41. The courier panted the news that both players were serving major penalties.

"Crimey," howled my Canadian companion, as he coughed the raw vodka through the gaps in his front teeth. "This must be the end of the world. Gilbert has gone berserk. We'd better get back into the arena so that we'll have a good seat when the bomb goes off."

Well, we got back to our seats soon enough to see Alan Eagleson logging more ice time than Don Awrey and Marcel Dionne have logged in the series. The Eagle flew down from his perch, screaming wildly, when the goal judge failed to turn on the red light as Yvan Cournoyer tied the score at 12:56. This was the same goal judge who flashed the red light only for a split second when Paul Henderson scored the winner in the sixth game on Tuesday night.

Anyhow, a full platoon of the Soviet militia grabbed Eagleson as he left his seat. They were giving him the heave-ho right out of the ruddy building when the Canadian hockey players, brandishing their hickory staves, converged on the boards, immediately adjacent to the spot where The Eagle was going down for the third time.

Peter Mahovlich vaulted the boards and plunged into that crowd of militia. The other Canadian players were ready to follow Pete when — suddenly and inexplicably — at least 10 militiamen retreated, leaving Eagleson resembling a pile of garbage. The players picked up Eagleson as, pale-faced and badly shaken, he was almost entirely a passenger while they propelled him clear across mid-ice to the other side of the rink and the security of the Canadian team's bench.

Never in the history of organized hockey has there been such an extraordinary spectacle. The Russian players and the Russian crowd stood in stunned silence as the Canadian hockey team took matters into their own rough hands.

Come to think of it, Eagleson, with his glasses dangling from one ear, was the centre of a scene which was absurdly reminiscent of Eliza and Little Eva fleeing across the ice in that famous hominy-and-grits melodrama, *Uncle Tom's Cabin*.

Eagleson's feet hadn't even dried out after his first trip across the ice when he had bounded over the boards again. This time, Alan and almost every member of the Canadian hockey contingent, from coach through civvy-clad non-playing members of the squad to physiotherapist and stick-boy, was slithering and sliding madly to converge on the doorstep of the Russian net, where Paul Henderson had just finished scoring the winning goal of the entire damn series at 19:26.

Once again, the same goal judge didn't flash the red light as Henderson picked up his own rebound and shoved the puck under shell-shocked Vladislav Tretiak. The two referees didn't need the glow of the red light to tell them that the puck was in the net. At least 30 Canadian lunatics were pointing at the puck. They were yelling deliriously and they were clouting Henderson until his skull was ringing like a Chinese gong.

These heroics are becoming old hat to Henderson. He scored the winning goal in each of the final three games as Canada rushed to a genuinely thrilling triumph in the unofficial world championship of hockey. As a matter of fact, Paul also scored the fourth Canadian goal — which should have been the winner — in last Friday's opening game on Moscow Ice. That was the simply revolting occasion on which the Canadian team suffered a six-minute defensive lapse in the third period and they blew a three-goal lead.

You and I have our own highly emotional opinion of the type of hockey entertainment that was provided in this eight-game series, but assistant coach John Ferguson probably expressed it for everyone. Bill Brennan, of the *Detroit Free Press* asked Fergy: "Did you ever see such a good hockey series?"

"Never, never," Ferguson replied firmly. Then, giving the matter approximately one second of thought, he said, in amendment: "Well, maybe that series two years ago, when we (Montreal Canadiens) beat Boston in the first round of the Stanley Cup playoffs."

In view of the fact that I haven't been backward in expressing my opinion over the past four weeks, I have a compulsion to add that, for me, never has there been another hockey show which has matched this one in sustained excitement.

Remember, for a moment, that this was a Canadian team which was beaten on its own home ice. Then, after being booed by some of their own nutty countrymen in Vancouver, these hockey players came all the way to unfamiliar Moscow and they beat the Russians before a partisan Russian crowd.

As our old horse-racing friend, defenceman Serge Savard, shouted in the dressing room last night, "a good race horse always comes from behind to win. We won like a good race horse. We did it the hard way — we came from behind."

"I thought that we had the series under control Tuesday night when we got some pretty good officiating from Dahlberg and Bata," growled Phil Esposito, who shared with Henderson the role of Canada's outstanding individual player over the series wearing himself to a shadow with his selfless display in the past month. "Then, tonight, we got that (obscenity) German as a referee and he damn nearly screws us out of the championship."

Mr. Esposito was referring to Mr. Josef Kompalla, a West German alleged hockey referee, who must be the last word in cloth-headed guffins. Kompalla almost penalized the Canadians out of the rink in the first period and the lid blew off when he gave Jean-Paul Parisé a very, very questionable interference penalty at 4:10.

Parisé lost his head when Kompalla added a misconduct penalty. Kompalla almost lost his head, too, because Parisé rushed at him with his stick raised high over his left shoulder and he acted as if he would decapitate the referee.

Kompalla ordered Parisé to the dressing room with a match penalty. Around the Canadian bench, the occupants almost went insane. In fact, a few did take leave of their senses: A Canadian threw a chair on to the ice, where it disintegrated. Some one else near the Canadian bench threw another chair on to the ice. For a moment, it appeared possible that coach Harry Sinden might take his team to the dressing room and refuse to finish the game.

Fortunately for the prestige of Canadian hockey, the game was continued to its successful conclusion. The Soviets were leading 1-0 at the time of Parise's expulsion. But it must be acknowledged that the display around the Canadian bench did little to enhance our reputation in world diplomatic circles.

I must confess that I shared a bit of the Canadian team's feelings of rancour. I felt that the Soviets took a dead set on us yesterday. The Russians, of course, controlled all the seat sales and last night, for the first time, they inserted an organized cheering section of approximately 300 persons, directly in the middle of the Canadian rooting section.

This Soviet "fifth column" did its level best to counteract the Canadian cheering. One stalwart girl had a Soviet flag which she waved violently every time the television cameras turned on the Canadian section.

I wish that you could have been in the rink with me. It was the damndest feeling, to stand there at the end of the game, listening to 3,000 Canadians, thousands of miles from home, singing O *Canada* as they glowed with pride. Then, they began to chant: "We're Number One, We're Number One."

I looked at the spot where the Russian infiltrators had been sitting among the Canadians. Every last one of them had disappeared within 30 seconds after the dramatic end of the game — flags and all.

One mild complaint: After lunch on Wednesday, Paul Henderson made a prediction that Ronnie Ellis would score the goal which would win the series for Canada. Paul Henderson is a fine hockey player, but as a prognosticator, he's a bum. Now, if ever you're looking for really valuable predictions, just read this column.

HENDERSON'S SUPERNATURAL TRICK

JIM TAYLOR

September 29, 1972 — *The Vancouver Sun*

MOSCOW — It will never go into the record books as a hat trick because record books are cold and dry and don't give a damn about drama. But Paul Henderson has the greatest hat trick in the history of hockey.

Three games — three uphill, grinding, incredible hockey games for Team Canada. Three straight one-goal victories over Russia to take their eight-game series 4-3-1. And three times, the winning goal triggered by Paul Henderson.

This is Paul Henderson after the clincher Thursday night, the one with 34 seconds left, the third of the period for Team Canada, the one that meant a 6-5 victory and the series.

"I saw the puck go under him, I knew it was going in and the only thing I could think of was 'Omigawd, we've done it.' And then I looked up because somebody up there must be doing something.

"Three game-winners, I tell you ... a thing like this ... for a kid from Kincardine ... oh boy ... that's all ... oh boy."

There were all sorts of side issues to this one, Alan Eagleson being grabbed by Russian police as he vaulted to the concourse to find out why the light didn't go on after Yvan Cournoyer's goal, Pete Mahovlich jumping over the boards to rescue him, the stupidity of chairs thrown to the ice from the vicinity of the Canadian bench, the irrational actions of Canadian fans when J. P. Parisé was so rightly ejected from the game. But the one over-riding thing, as it has been since Team Canada staggered in from Sweden, has been the hockey itself.

This has been a series with two winners. Team Canada won the series, but the wildest Canadian nationalist can't overlook the fact that the Russians won their point.

Over eight games against the cream of the National Hockey League — eight hours of the best hockey you'll ever hope to see — the Soviets outscored Team Canada 32-31. Or put is this way: What would you have said to a suggestion before the series that going into the third period of the final game Team Canada would be praying for two goals to get a tie in game and series? The Russians said they'd stack up against the best hockey players in the world. And they found out. So did we.

We found out a lot of things.

We found out we no longer have the only game in town. We found out that there is something more in a pro player's heart than a cash register and a recording that says "What's in it for me?"

We found out that international hockey — the game itself — is better than ours. Now we find out if we're smart enough to accept it. We found out that if our athletes are to compete in the world market they'll have to stop training like stamina is a speech impediment.

"I knew we could beat these guys once we got in shape," said Ron Ellis, the tireless checker of the Henderson line. "It just took us half the series to get there."

A dispassionate observer might ask why.

We found out, too, that there are players on this Russian team who could play for anybody, anytime, anywhere. People rave about Valeri Kharlamov, and he is a brilliant stick-handler with speed to burn. But there isn't an NHL owner around who wouldn't give what's left of his soul to grab large, superbly talented Alexander Yakushev, who scored two more last night to tie Henderson and Esposito for the series lead at seven.

Naturally, there'll have to be a rematch, and the argument will rage for months whether it should be an all-star team or a club team, and when and where it should be played. But those are details.

What matters is that on a world scale or a scale of pure entertainment, this will rank with the greatest series ever played. It cries for an encore, and no matter whose flag we wave, we all come up winners.

NEW YEAR'S EVE BASH

RED FISHER

September 23, 2004 — *The Gazette (Montreal)*

ALMOST 29 YEARS after The Game, people are still calling it the greatest ever played. It had all of the ingredients: the Stanley Cup champion Canadiens playing at their best against the Central Red Army team with all of its great stars from the 1972 Summit Series. Who could ask for more, eh?

Question: Does it even come close to that accolade? When the Canadiens outshoot the Soviets 38-13 in a 3-3 skirmish, holding them to four shots in the first period, three in the second and six in the third, they were as near-perfect as any team can be. Call it a highlight-reel game for the Canadiens, but when the most important position on any hockey team springs leaks, "greatest" is hardly the word for it.

It's not that Ken Dryden wasn't prepared for this exhibition. In the hours before it, he did all of the right things.

Friends and relatives had started to arrive for the much-anticipated 1975 New Year's Eve game, so the Canadiens goaltender checked into a downtown hotel to avoid distractions. His head was clear and he was well-rested during the team warmup.

Early in the second period, he stopped doing all of the right things.

If he had played like the Dryden who had gone into the game with a remarkable 1.79 goals-against average in his first 31 games of the NHL season, he would not have been beaten three times on 13 shots — two of the goals coming early and late from the Red Army's three second-period shots. If he had been vintage Dryden, he would not have allowed the only goal of the third period, during which the Canadiens outshot the Soviets 16-6 in a mismatch that had them holding a 2-0 lead fewer than eight minutes into the game and a 3-1 lead midway through the second period.

The stunned Forum crowd knew it. Dryden knew it.

Much later, after a dejected Dryden had faced a blizzard of questions from a media horde, only he and a longtime newspaper friend were at his dressing-room stall.

"Happy New Year, Ken," he was told.

"Same to you," he said with a heavy sigh.

"You screwed up, pal," I said.

"I'm disappointed ... very disappointed," Dryden said. "I don't believe in luck ... good or bad. You make your own. The team played so well. Everybody ... but on the first goal (Boris Mikhailov) and on the third (Boris Aleksandrov), the puck hits the base of my hand, falls to the ice and then rolls over the line. I can remember so many times when the puck fell and just stayed there. That's what was so disappointing.

"The last couple of days haven't been easy, you know," he added. "So many things on our minds ... but we played so well. I wish I could have done better."

Dryden, the player, never took defeat or criticism lightly, so for this Hall of Fame goaltender to say: "I wish I could have done better" is as far as he's ever gone to admit he hadn't brought his "A" game that night.

The Habs deserved infinitely better, because on this night they made the Soviet Superman Theory look like Swiss cheese. Holes everywhere.

What was it everybody was saying about the Brothers Kharlamov?

— They skate too fast for NHL opposition. Wrong. They were outskated from start to finish.

— They control the puck in their zone. The fact is, the Soviets made errant passes all night. That couldn't have been Alexsandr Gusev, Vladimir Lutchenko and Valeri Vasiliev piling error upon error.

— Don't take penalties, because the Soviet power play is deadly. Hmph! Three times they held man advantages, yet didn't get a shot against the fierce-checking Canadiens.

— They don't miss scoring opportunities, scoring on their fifth, seventh and ninth shots, but a Dryden playing reasonably well would not have allowed more than one goal.

— Soviet goaltending (see Vladislav Tretiak) is brilliant. No argument. If anything, that was an understatement on this holiday night. He was incredible, at times. The stops he made against Jacques Lemaire during the first and last minutes of the third period were astonishing.

How lopsided was this game? Steve Shutt and Yvon Lambert were the Canadiens' goal-scorers before the game was eight minutes old, while the Soviets didn't get their first shot until 9:46. Yvan Cournoyer lifted his colleagues into a 3-1 lead midway through the second. Still, coach Scott Bowman — who hated to lose or even tie — was grinning from earlobe to earlobe after it was over.

"How's that for a team effort?" he asked. "This team was ready. This team worked. This team did everything it had to do. It's true we should have won, and that's a little disappointing. I'm proud of this team."

He had to be proud of kids like Doug Risebrough, Mario Tremblay, Lambert, Doug Jarvis and Bob Gainey. He had to be proud of the entire defence corps, Serge Savard, in particular.

Bowman, of course, knew that better goaltending would have won. "Ken didn't get much work. All right ... he wasn't great, but those things happen."

He also knew that anything less than Tretiak's brilliance would have provided the Canadiens with at least a half-dozen goals. So did players such as Guy Lapointe.

"They told us how much better-conditioned the Soviets are," Lapointe said. "Maybe they are, but I played this game and didn't feel tired for a minute. Most of the time we had to wait for them. We didn't have to chase them. The score doesn't say so, but everybody knows which was the much better team."

The Canadiens went into the game dedicated to applying pressure in the Red Army's zone, and it returned early dividends on the Shutt and Lambert goals. The remarkable thing about the game plan, though, was its exquisite execution. The Soviets were allowed only one three-on-two break and one two-on-one situation during the entire game and scored each time — with shots that should have been stopped.

THE SOVIETS CAN'T BEAT OUR BEST

JIM COLEMAN

January 12, 1976 — *Southam News*

PHILADELPHIA — The National Hockey League salvaged a modicum of its tattered pride yesterday afternoon when Philadelphia Flyers, holders of the Stanley Cup the past two seasons, whomped Soviet Central Army 4-1. Unquestionably, the Soviets were the overall winners of this eight-game series. But the NHL can boast defiantly that the Russian all-stars still are incapable of defeating North America's three best professional teams — Philadelphia Flyers, Montreal Canadiens and Buffalo Sabres.

The emotionally supercharged Flyers rescued the NHL from possible humiliation with a carefully planned, flawlessly executed display of forechecking and exceptionally rugged positional hockey which, in the first period of yesterday's game, came perilously close to the boundary line of intimidation.

There isn't the slightest doubt the Soviets were "hearing footsteps" in that first period. Even the stoutest-hearted of the Army skaters were throwing snow as the Flyers bumped them, harried them and kept them hemmed within the Russian defensive zone. If those tactics alone weren't sufficient to inhibit the Soviets, certainly they must have been awed by the crazy spectators whose blood calls produced utter bedlam within the Spectrum.

By North American professional standards, this wasn't a particularly rough game, but the Central Army team never before had been exposed to the Flyers' copyrighted brand of physical attrition. The vigour with which they were being checked impelled them to stalk indignantly from the ice and stage a 14-minute walkout at 11:21 of the first period. Shades of Andrei Gromyko at the United Nations.

The incident which precipitated the walkout was a shoulder check with which Ed Van Impe flattened fleet Valeri Kharlamov in the Philadelphia defensive zone. Only 11 seconds earlier Van Impe had jumped back on the ice after serving a rather unnecessary penalty for spilling Alexander Maltsev. As Eddie swarmed into the defensive zone to assist his beleaguered teammates, Kharlamov had his head down as he attempted to accept a pass. Van Impe hit him with a solid check and Kharlamov won another Academy Award as he swooned to the ice and lay there, obviously *in extremis*. When the Soviet trainer had carefully re-inflated Valeri with a bicycle pump, the Soviet delegation withdrew, sulking, while the Spectrum spectators showered them with quaint vocal maledictions.

It was only when they were informed they might forfeit their share of the gate receipts that the Russians returned to the ice. Obviously, this North American tour wasn't entirely a goodwill mission — the Soviet delegation scarcely dare to return to Moscow without those stacks of nice crisp U.S. and Canadian currency.

Referee Lloyd Gilmour and Van Impe later confirmed the press box suspicions that there had been nothing illegal about the check which dismantled the haughty and colourful Kharlamov.

"I came out of the penalty box at full speed," Eddie said later in his team's noisy dressing room. "Kharlamov had his head down, looking for the puck. My right shoulder hit him flush on the left cheek. It was a good shot, but it wasn't as solid as that guy made it look when he dropped to the ice."

Personally, I believe the Soviet walkout was the direct result of frustration. I never thought I'd see the day when an individual NHL team could check the Central Army so thoroughly that the Russians would be forced out of their game plan. But the Flyers thoroughly spooked the Russians. They forced the Soviets to play "the Philadelphia game," and the Flyers were the unquestioned masters of that hockey technique. Coach Fred Shero's two-and-a-half years of studying Russian game films produced a result that warmed the heart of every Canadian hockey fanatic.

Let me, for instance, remind you how the Flyers completely nullified the Central Army's normally fearsome power play. Four times between the seven-minute mark of the first period and the 3:08 mark of the second the Flyers were left shorthanded by minor penalties. That makes a total of eight minutes that Philadelphia played five against six in the early stages of the game. But, in those entire eight minutes, the Russians didn't get *a single shot on the Philadelphia net.*

And throughout those eight minutes, coach Konstantin Loktev was relying almost constantly on his clever trio of Kharlamov, Boris Mikhailov and Maltsev who, in those situations, usually fill the opposing net with smoking pucks.

The Philadelphia defenders were supremely competent during those crises. Seldom did they permit the Soviets to approach goalie Wayne Stephenson. The Flyers outshot the Central Army 49-13 over the 60-minute route, and many a time yesterday afternoon, the Flyer marksmen shot without taking aim. Then, that rascal Vladislav Tretiak stood between them and success. If Tretiak was brilliant against the Montreal Canadiens and the Boston Bruins, he attained even greater heights yesterday.

Let me close with a few words about our old friend Stephenson. This victory was, for him, particularly sweet. Wayne toiled in the nets of Canada's national team for three seasons and the Russians were his nemesis.

He was beaming happily yesterday as Canadian reporters congratulated him in the Philly dressing room. "I think we beat them twice in all the years the national team played against them; in the 1967 Centennial tournament at Winnipeg and once in the Izvestia tournament in Russia. But, this really was something else. It was nice to play against them behind this particular team."

Then, as a man who has finally been avenged for many indignities, Stephenson added: "If this Soviet Army team played regularly in the NHL, they wouldn't last two weeks."

Oh, well ... he doesn't *really* believe that, but who can begrudge him his moment of over-exultation?

SKALBANIA SIGNS YOUNG GRETZKY

JIM MATHESON

June 12, 1978 — *The Edmonton Journal*

THE BOY WONDER sat in the crowded private jet of Nelson Skalbania fingering a cheque for $30,000 — a mere down payment on a seven-year personal services contract worth, conservatively, $1.75 million.

"I guess the master plan worked," shrugged Wayne Gretzky as he talked to the *Journal* in an exclusive interview Sunday afternoon at the Municipal Airport. "The dream's come true...."

The teenager from Brantford — the most touted young hockey player, the most eagerly anticipated genius of the national game since Bobby Orr — is suddenly a millionaire at 17.

In a whirlwind round of negotiations, Skalbania pulled off the coup of the decade — and opened warfare with the NHL — by signing the underage centre "to so much money my banker might cut off my credit.

"I'm not going to give you the exact figure," said Skalbania, firing the first volley in what figures to be all-out hostility between the leagues. "It's a bundle ... at least $1 million for the first four years."

Gretzky, who scored 182 points last season with the Sault Ste. Marie Greyhounds of the Ontario Hockey Association at $75 a week, will work for Skalbania wherever he goes. Currently, Skalbania is the majority owner of the Indianapolis Racers of the World Hockey Association. But there is a possibility that he could purchase the struggling Houston Aeros, too.

"Heck ... maybe he'll just be a deckhand on my boat in the Mediterranean," laughed Skalbania, the former owner of the Edmonton Oilers.

The signing — completed on a flight from Vancouver to Edmonton with Gretzky's agent Gus Badali and his parents Walter and Phyllis Gretzky — was precipitated by Skalbania's dislike for the owners of the National Hockey League. He wanted to hit them below the belt, and it looks like he's succeeded.

"I don't really know if this will kill any talk of merger between the two leagues now or not," said Skalbania, who doesn't figure to be in on one, anyway, as owner of Indianapolis. "I do know I didn't like going on my hands and knees begging to get into the NHL last year. Maybe they'll call a truce now and say enough is enough. The situation now is just ridiculous."

Skalbania said the NHL's greed in stealing WHA free agents (Ulf Nilsson, Anders Hedberg and Dan Labraaten, all of Winnipeg) without compensation to the WHA was one of the things that forced his hand.

"I see no other alternative but to sign underage juniors and sign the best of them," said Skalbania, intimating that his fellow WHA partners could go on a binge now and sign up to 20 youngsters.

Gretzky wasn't the first exceptional player signed by a WHA club, of course. Toronto Toros grabbed Marlie juniors Wayne Dillon and Mark Napier, Houston went for Mark Howe and John Tonelli and New England for Gordie Roberts.

But the Gretzky Success Story is straight out of Hollywood. He started skating when he was only 2 — almost before he could say "pass the Pablum." His dad, Walter, a teletype operator for Bell Canada, built a rink in the family backyard in Brantford, Ontario. In keeping with the script, Wayne was a media darling while still in kindergarten.

The reporters discovered him when he was only five and he made the Brantford novice all-star team — a squad usually made up of 10- and 11-year-olds. That led to local TV exposure at six, a feature story in a major Canadian daily newspaper at eight and a *Hockey Night in Canada* film clip at nine — a mini-legend at 11.

He scored 378 goals in 68 games, including three in 45 seconds in the third period of a game in which Brantford trailed 3-0. Three years later, he was playing Junior B hockey against guys 19 and 20. When he finally made it to Junior A as a 16-year-old in the Soo, he naturally scored a hat trick in his first game. Last Christmas he topped it off by leading all scorers in the world junior tournament in Montreal.

Skalbania picked the night before the NHL summer meetings to announce he'd signed Gretzky. The timing was a blockbuster.

"Personally, I think you've got to fight fire with fire," said Skalbania. "I don't see why we (in the WHA) have to sit back like nice guys and hope the NHL gives us a call concerning a merger or marriage. We got raped last year when we had to show them our books and make so many concessions like giving up TV revenue and draft choices."

Skalbania thinks the "mental giants" in the NHL are walking around with "blinkers on. A merger would solve all matters. Right now the WHA is costing each NHL team about $1 million more a year to operate because they've had to give kids huge signing bonuses and up player salaries to the moon. That's $18 million a year. If there was only one league they'd each save $1 million — the break-even point for over half the teams in the NHL."

Skalbania says the fans are getting it in the neck more than anyone because of the war between the leagues.

"The NHL fans pay $1.50 to $2.50 more per seat per game because we're in business."

Skalbania said a first-round draft pick in this year's junior lottery later this week will command "a $200,000 signing bonus plus $150,000 or so a year for five years." According to the Indy owner these salaries are "totally unrealistic. They can't possibly be amortized by the game of hockey today. A merger would mean a signing bonus for a kid of $20,000 and perhaps $50,000 a year for five years."

CHERRY LOSES
WITH CLASS

AL STRACHAN

May 11, 1979 — The Gazette (Montreal)

(Editor's note: A bench penalty for too many men on the ice cost the Boston Bruins a berth in the 1979 Stanley Cup final, and eventually cost coach Don Cherry his job. Twenty-six years later, the incident is all most people remember about Cherry's coaching career — but he found a sympathetic ear that night in the Gazette's *Al Strachan. This sidebar gives an early glimpse of Cherry in full, pre-Coach's Corner bluster.)*

A TIRED, OBVIOUSLY shaken Don Cherry still held his head high.

Resplendent in a blue-suede jacket and a light-green vest and trousers, he climbed up on a chair a few minutes after his Bruins had gone down to a heartbreaking defeat to the Canadiens.

"I feel like crying for (the Boston players) — I really do," he said. "Not for me. For them. I'm so proud of them. I'm as proud of my players as he (Canadiens coach Scotty Bowman) is of his. Cash (Wayne Cashman) had to have a shot to kill the pain before the game. So did Schmautzie (Bobby Schmautz), Brad Park and a couple of others. It's very disappointing.

"I don't know how you can get more disappointed than being ahead 3-1 in the third period, being ahead 4-3 with less than two minutes to play and losing in overtime."

It's a shame to see it happen to an honest, hard-working guy like Cherry. He has done a tremendous job with his team and received no thanks from his employers. And yet, here he was, moments after an excruciatingly painful loss, talking to reporters who, by the very nature of their vocation, don't make things any easier. He did it with class, and even a sense of humour.

When asked about the crucial penalty for too many men on the ice in the final minutes which gave the Canadiens a power play, he said, "That was my fault. Any time you get too many men on the ice it's the coach's fault."

Then he chuckled. "Hell, I grabbed two of them or there would have been *eight* of them on the ice."

But he couldn't resist a dig at the Canadiens, who tend to be of the opinion that they're too important to talk to the media during the playoffs. When asked by one of the local reporters if he could go into the Bruins' dressing room, Cherry said, "Not yet. Give them a minute. What are you, a sadist? Why don't you go over to the victors' side? Now that they've won the series, they've probably got a lot to say. Just remember who's been talking to you for seven games."

And although that kind of shot may not sound like it, Cherry does respect the Canadiens. "What a shot he let go," he said of Guy Lafleur, the man he calls "the greatest hockey player in the world now that Himself (Bobby Orr) has retired."

But don't get the idea that Cherry is in love with the Canadiens. When asked who he hoped would win the final series between the Rangers and Canadiens, Cherry stonefacedly said: "That's like asking me to choose between syphillis and gonhorrea."

And when pressed, he finally unloaded on the officiating. The first few questions he judiciously avoided. After all, the league threatened to fine him $10,000 if he criticized the officials during the playoffs. But finally, he could keep it in no longer.

"Nice, eh?" he asked. "Isn't that sweet?

"Tiger Williams in Toronto gets a penalty in overtime. We get two in the third period. I could see it coming when it was 3-1. I was just waiting. I know how Williams feels now. But I'm not going to complain about the officiating. I think any game is bad when we lose."

45

THE GREATEST!

'What he did was absolutely amazing.'
— FLYERS' GOALIE PETE PEETERS

TERRY JONES

December 31, 1981 — *The Edmonton Journal*

TODAY THE ROCKET'S Red Glare looks more like a mere flick of a Bic.

When it comes to lighting up a league, and the goal lights therein, now there's Wayne Gretzky and once you've said that, you've said it all.

Make no mistake. It wasn't just another Great Gretzky game last night. It was the greatest hockey game ever played by the greatest player in the history of the game — to break the greatest record ever set in the game. Nothing less than that.

Five in one night to do it! Nine in the last two nights! Fifty in 39! Forget the adjectives.

Wayne Gretzky didn't just break Rocket Richard's 50-goals-in-50-games. He annihilated it. And I would hope, today, that it is unanimous — especially in every old folks home where they talk in reverent tones of the six-team NHL. There's no way anyone can ridicule the record because of expansion and the style of play and all the other sacred excuses. The Kid made sure of that.

And there's no way anybody can carp that he scored No. 50 into an empty net. Not when it was the fifth goal of the game and in Game 39. Besides, it just might rate as the most exciting empty-net goal in history. In all, what happened last night was more than hockey history. It was one of hockey history's most magic moments of all time. Last night will be, at least until the Oilers win a Stanley Cup, The Game I'll Never Forget.

Gretzky's not in much of a position to compare his record to The Rocket's because he wasn't born when The Rocket set it and he can't remember watching any six-team NHL games on TV, although he recalls seeing Rocket Richard on a between-periods interview once.

"All I can say is that I believe hockey is better now than it was, say, 15 years ago. I think the players are bigger and better. And 15 years from now, I think they'll be better than we are. Everything improves."

And from here? The mind, as always, boggles.

"I think I can double everything," said Gretzky. That's 100 goals and 216 points.

"As long as the rest of the guys on the team keep playing the way they are, I think I'm capable of doubling what I've done so far."

Fifty goals in 39 games? One hundred and eight points in 39 games? One hundred and fifty-six goals and a total of 409 points in two-and-a-half NHL seasons? Two hundred and two goals and 519 points, including his year in the WHA?

There's one day left in this calendar year and with three periods to go in 1981 Gretzky has scored 95 goals with 142 assists for 237 points! That's the one record even Gretzky won't break.

That determination showed in every move last night. Never have so many gone through so much anguish with a player having the greatest game of his life. He'd already scored three halfway through the second period and the fans were so restless it was unbelievable.

When he scored No. 49, the standing ovation compared with the win over the Canadiens in the playoff series last year. They began, this crowd that expects the impossible — for the first time ever — to chant "Gretzky-Gretzky-Gretzky." They'd chanted "Guy-Guy-Guy" for Lafleur in the Canada Cup and "Andy-Andy-Andy" in the playoffs for goalie Andy Moog, but never before had Gretzky so incredibly performed the impossible that his name would be repeated over and over.

The greatest game he ever played?

Don't take it from me. Take it from Gretzky himself. Normally, Gretzky gives it the old Dizzy Dean approach of "You rate 'em, I'll score 'em." But last night, in his still amazingly modest way, he said: "It probably was."

Certainly, he admitted, while he didn't feel it rated with the team thrill of beating the Montreal Canadiens in the playoffs last year, it was THE special moment, from an individual point of view, in his career.

"I guess I'm more delighted with this than anything," he said.

"People are now going to have to re-evaluate their stars of the century," was how Oilers coach Glen Sather put it. And then he added, "I don't think we've seen the best of Wayne yet."

The Greatest! And still just a kid.

UNBELIEVEABLE:
MR. WAYNEDERFUL NEEDED FIVE GOALS FOR THE FASTEST 50 IN HISTORY — AND GOT THEM ALL

JIM MATHESON

December 31, 1981 — The Edmonton Journal

BOBBY CLARKE SLUMPED on a bench in the Philadelphia Flyer dressing room, his face a mixture of wonder and fright.

"This is absolutely crazy," said the Flyers' playing coach, trying to put words to Wayne Gretzky's out-of-this-world feat of 50 goals in 39 NHL games. "At least with (Bobby) Orr, you'd see him wind up in his own end and you could try to set up some kind of defence to stop him. Gretzky just comes out of nowhere ... it's scary."

Gretzky skated into the NHL record book Wednesday with five goals as the Oilers held off the Flyers 7-5 in an NHL shoot-out. He scored them from every possible angle — once when a puck bounced off the backboards, one on a breakaway, two on blistering shots from between the face-off circles, the last into an empty net.

When the last one went in, Gretzky was buried under teammates along the corner-boards, the roar of 17,490 fans ringing in his ears. It was almost, but not quite, the highlight of his NHL career. "It's the second-best feeling I've ever had ... it's not quite as thrilling as beating Montreal in the playoffs last year," said Gretzky.

Yet, the unbelievable quality of the feat was the same in both. Only this was an individual thing — a race to destroy a record held by Rocket Richard

(1944-45) and Mike Bossy (1980-81).

"Things like this aren't supposed to happen," said Oiler defenceman Paul Coffey. "He's had nine goals in two straight games (he had four vs. Los Angeles Sunday) yet, when he sets a goal for himself, he gets it, it's that simple. He wanted to do it by the 40th game. You could have bet $1 million against him doing it, but I knew he would."

Coffey wasn't the only supporter in his corner either. Gretzky's roomie Kevin Lowe knew an explosion might be coming. He knew it hours before the game when the two were sitting down to bacon and eggs — cooked by Gretzky.

"He said there was no reason why he couldn't score five against the Flyers," said Lowe.

Gretzky said before the season that Phil Esposito's 76 goals in 78 games in 1970-71 was the record that might stand forever. Now, he's not so sure — not at the pace he's been going. "That's a tough one," admitted Gretzky, who's now scored in nine straight games — 18 goals in that span. "That's still 26 goals in the last 40 games (actually 41). I scored only 21 in 40 (his first 40 last season)."

Nobody is going to say it's impossible. Certainly not Oilers coach Glen Sather, who had only 80 goals in his entire NHL career.

"I hope he passes me in one year," said Sather.

OILERS QUENCH AN OLD THIRST

JIM MATHESON

May 20, 1984 — *The Edmonton Journal*

Oilers 5 Islanders 2
Edmonton wins Stanley Cup 4-1

TURN ON THE lights, the party's starting.

The Edmonton Oilers' thirst for a first Stanley Cup was quenched Saturday when they danced to hockey's national anthem, *We Are The Champions*, in concert with *The Impossible Dream* — their theme song three years ago when they first became Canada's Team with a shocking playoff win over the Montreal Canadiens.

The New York Islanders' Drive For Five ran out of gas as Wayne Gretzky scored twice on Billy Smith, sending the fans' Public Enemy No. 1 to the bench after just 20 minutes — the second time Smith had been yanked in the three Oiler wins at Northlands Coliseum.

Ken Linseman and Jari Kurri greeted reliever Rollie Melanson with two goals in his first four shots, but Isles' coach Al Arbour couldn't go to his bullpen for Kelly Hrudey, the third goalie. He wasn't dressed. Smith and Melanson were both on the bench when Dave Lumley made it hysteria-city with an 180-footer into the heart of an empty net in the dying seconds.

The Isles didn't go quietly into the night, though. They came to the party late, but Pat LaFontaine scored twice in the first 35 seconds of the third period to temporarily silence the 17,498 invited guests.

In the end, Gretzky was carrying the silver mug over his head in jubilation, though, his five cars and 200 black-and-white TVs as Toyota player of the week and year, his Art Ross (scoring title) and Hart (MVP) awards forgotten for the moment.

A disco dance celebrated the second youngest National Hockey League franchise ever to win the Cup; the New York Rangers won in 1940, their third NHL year.

The Oilers took five seasons — just as owner Peter Pocklington had forecast. "I was pretty naive when I said it on a show with Dick Beddoes, and maybe Glen Sather was, too, but the players believed it," said Peter Puck.

Pocklington was drenched in champagne, the memory of the hockey win and the bet he made with Islanders owner John Pickett fresh in his mind. "You'll never know how much I won," he said, "and I got odds."

Gretzky's eyes were misty, the result of a bubbly bath and the thrill of the moment.

"It's exciting to win individual awards," said Gretzky, who's won everything imaginable in his five NHL years — except something from *Ring* magazine.

"But there's no feeling like this. Nothing compares. When I was carrying the Cup, I thought of Jean Beliveau. I remembered when he picked it up, how good he looked with it. I was worried about dropping it, though. I told Coff (Paul Coffey) to get behind me to help me out."

Gretzky made an impassioned speech before the game, telling his teammates that all his individual baubles meant nothing unless he got the Cup.

"I told him none of mine did, either," joked Dave Semenko, whose lasting impression of the Stanley Cup victory lap was "the Cup was lighter than I thought."

Semenko, who's been an Oiler longer than anybody, back to 1977, bathed in the memories of seven years.

"You always have doubts, but I've been with this bunch for so long that you've got to believe," he said. "We got close last year, got a taste of it, now we've got the Cup for at least a year. And nobody can take it from us."

Islanders captain Denis Potvin, who carried the Cup for four straight years in a victory dance, wasn't bitter about the reign ending.

"I felt no shame turning the Cup over to them. I'm damn' proud ... several Oilers talked about idolizing us as we shook hands. One great team turning it over to a team that was great all year. They deserved it," said Potvin.

Oilers defenceman Kevin Lowe, who was in the running for the Conn Smythe Trophy won by housemate Mark Messier, was riding a wave of emotions. "From the time I was a kid, I have always thought that the neatest thing about the Stanley Cup would be standing up there on national TV, somebody pouring champagne over your head. Darned if it didn't happen," said Lowe.

The Oilers outscored the Islanders 19-6 in the three games at Northlands, running their gaudy home record this season to 44-7-1. Gretzky's two goals and an assist on Kurri's powerplay 40-footer gave him 35 points in the playoffs — seven against the Isles. All of them came in the three games here, where he finally broke out of his slump.

"I never doubted Wayne. He was playing under a lot of pressure but he showed his true form, what a leader he is," said Semenko, of Gretzky's two first-period scores on Smith — one on a breakaway, the other on a three-on-one break.

After second-period goals by Kurri and Linseman, the Oilers took a comfortable 4-0 lead into the final period, but LaFontaine struck twice on the first shift of the third.

What was Andy Moog thinking when the tide seemed to be turning?

"I was just happy he didn't get a third one," said the Oilers goalie. "The first one was a nice play, the second was a lucky one, off his skate."

Lumley ended the suspense with his long shot into the empty net.

"Right in the middle," crowed the right winger. "But then, I'm a solid six-goal-a-year scorer, so it was expected, right? Actually, I was wondering if it was even going to count. I looked over at Mark and he had his hands in the air and his gloves off. I thought the game was over."

Oilers winger Dave Hunter, who missed the last two games with a bruised spleen and sore ribs, came slip-sliding onto the ice to join the celebration.

"It was a great feeling until somebody came up behind me and crushed my ribs," winced Hunter. "Still, I can live with that, eh?"

WHAT A THRILLER: TEAM CANADA CAPTURES FABULOUS SERIES ON GRETZKY-TO-LEMIEUX WINNING GOAL

PETE McMARTIN

September 16, 1987 — *The Vancouver Sun*

HAMILTON — Michel Goulet falls back on the locker room bench, pours champagne over Brian Propp's head, and as if he has just made a joyous discovery, howls: "This is hockey!"

Outside Copps Coliseum, Hamiltonians pour out onto the street and throw a night-long party. They indulge in an unabashed display of national pride. Honking horns. Waving hundreds of Canadian flags. Spontaneously breaking into choruses of *O Canada*!

Returning to his hotel alone, Soviet defenceman Igor Kravchuk is stopped by a pretty girl as he enters the elevator. She asks for his autograph. Morosely, he signs his name. Then another fan asks him for his autograph, and another and another. He signs a half-dozen autographs before he retreats to the solitude of the open elevator, but not before a man pats him gently on the back and says, "Great game, man."

What Canadians witnessed Tuesday night in that 6-5 thriller was the culmination of the greatest hockey series yet played. It had a happy ending if you happened to be Canadian. But even the Soviets agreed they had never witnessed anything like it.

"It was the greatest hockey I have ever seen played," said assistant coach Igor Dmitriev.

Team Canada defenceman Raymond Bourque put it another way. "If you saw an NHL game tomorrow, I think you'd realize the level of the game it was. I don't want to compare the NHL and the Canada Cup because they're two different things, but what you saw tonight was nothing like I've ever seen."

What we saw:

We saw the Soviets come flying out of their own end and stun the sell-out crowd by scoring in the first 26 seconds. Vladimir Krutov feeds Sergei Makarov a perfect pass from behind the Canadian net, and Makarov slaps it in.

We saw two more unanswered Soviet goals at 7:04 and 8:00 in the first period, the first on a slapshot by Alexei Gusarov, the second a beautiful individual effort by Viacheslav Fetisov, who skates around two Canadian defencemen and flips the puck over the sprawling Grant Fuhr. Fuhr looks shaky, the Canadian defence looks embarrassed, the future looks bleak.

We saw the Canadians slowly claw their way back. Previously unheralded players like Dale Hawerchuk, Rick Tocchet, Brent Sutter and Larry Murphy tenderize the Soviets with crunching body checks and chase them off the puck. Mark Messier hits Krutov with a bodycheck at the Canadian blue line that sends Krutov six feet off his feet. It initiates a new phase in the course of the game. Momentum swings toward the Canadians. Tocchet scores at 9:50 on a power play in the first, Propp scores at 15:23. Andrei Khomutov scores late in the first for the Soviets, making the first period score 4-2, but the Canadians are back in the game.

We saw a second period totally dominated by the Canadians. Scores by Murphy, Sutter and Hawerchuk put the Canadians past the Soviets. The fifth Canadian goal typifies the period, with Sutter slamming a Soviet defenceman into the boards behind the Soviet net, Hawerchuk picking up the loose puck, then spinning around the net and slapping at two rebounds until the third shot dribbles in.

And then we saw the third period, the climax to the best hockey ever played. Alexander Semak, the unknown rookie who scored the winning overtime goal in the first game in Montreal, ties it up at 12:21. Another overtime game, we thought.

But no. This game needed an end to fit its stature. After a faceoff in the Canadian end, who else but Wayne Gretzky could lead a four-on-two break against the Soviets in the last two minutes of play? Who else but Mario Lemieux could follow, and break into the open after Igor Stelnov falls? Of course, the pass Gretzky feeds Lemieux is perfect. Of course, the shot Lemieux takes is perfect, swift, and high to the glove side. Game.

"When I saw Gretzky and Lemieux go down the wing," Soviet coach Dmitriev said, "I understood it was the end of the game."

If anyone was still under the impression that this series was just another international hockey tournament, all they had to do was look at the celebration on the ice. It lasted 15 minutes, a chaotic, joyous milling of players and fans that rivalled any Stanley Cup finale. Gretzky and Hawerchuk lofted a Canadian flag while the Soviets looked on, standing silently at their blue line.

Afterwards, in the Canadian dressing room, the floor lay flooded with champagne. The Canada Cup, which is not a cup at all but a jagged, silver slab, stood ignored on top of a locker while players celebrated.

"Oh, man," Doug Crossman said, taking a swig of beer. "I'll tell you, there was a feeling in the air we were going to win tonight. We just felt it. And these guys are great. I've spent the best six weeks of my life here. The best six weeks of my hockey life."

Gretzky is asked about the team's feeling after the disastrous first period.

"That was a great period for the Soviets, but we had a lot of scoring chances, and I told the guys it could have been 3-3 rather than 4-2. I said 'Guys, don't worry about it. We'll come back.' I don't know the exact word to describe it, pride maybe, or determination, but Canadian teams have always had that ability to dig back from being behind. This is that kind of team."

Rick Tocchet: "It's got to be one of the greatest comebacks ever. We weren't worried about tying the game after that first period. We just wanted to keep it close. We knew that behind the net we could out-muscle them, so we took them to the boards there and coughed up a lot of pucks. If you remember, we scored a few goals from there."

Old-fashioned intimidation worked against the Soviets this game. "We banged them around during the second period," Hawerchuk said. "And we had their defencemen looking over their shoulder a few times."

"Everybody did their jobs tonight," Sutter said. "They came out flying and got a couple of goals on us. We came back by going to the body and forcing some things."

Does Canada's victory last night mean they are the greatest hockey team in the world?

The question is put to Dmitriev. He avoids the question, but agrees Canada did beat the Soviets in this tournament. "On a larger European hockey rink, played in Europe, the result could be different."

Besides, he says, the Soviet team must now prepare for the Olympics and the world championships.

Surely, a reporter says, he is not suggesting the competition the Soviets will find in the Olympics will be better than Team Canada.

Well, Dmitriev says, there is Sweden.

But Canada beat you, the reporter says. Sweden did not.

"Yes," he says without a hint of irony, "but Sweden is world champion."

Not in Hamilton, they're not.

ANCIENT EDIFICE PULLS THE PLUG

CAM COLE

May 25, 1988 — The Edmonton Journal

BOSTON — "Welcome, ladies and gentlemen," said the public address announcer, "to ... *historic* ... Boston Garden!"

Well, whatever else you want to call this claustrophobic old dump built on top of a train station, you have to admit it's historic.

A hockey team with a philosolphy that hasn't budged since the 1940s — except for one brief period when Bobby Orr budged it all by himself — plays here. So does the most famous basketball team in all creation, a team that wins with a slow male Caucasian who can't run or jump but still plays a pretty decent game of hoops.

And the building helps them all prosper. Boston teams win here.

They know its ins and outs, its shallow corners and its slow ice and its parquet floor, they learn to use the withering heat and the fans that hang over the nets, three levels stacked on top of one another.

And of course, visiting teams have to dress in a hellhole. That doesn't hurt.

Rats play here, too, it is said — real ones, not just Ken Linseman — though neither type has been much in evidence this week.

And there are nooks and crannies here where beer and urine and human sweat have penetrated, where paint can never reach, so that this frowsy old hothouse won't ever be anything but an anachronism — for all time, or as long as they let it stand.

And of all the reasons they let it stand, only two matter: (1) a new one would cost money, and (2) if they built a new one, the Boston teams probably wouldn't do so well.

Ah, but ladies and gentlemen, welcome to historic National Hockey League bylaw No. 27.12. The NHL invoked it Tuesday night, when the building tried just a little too hard to help out.

First, the Garden threw a six-foot pall of fog over the whole ice surface, so that referee Denis Morel had to ask the players from both benches to skate circles on it, to dissipate the haze, five separate times. But each time, it settled back a few moments later. Thicker.

"You could feel it on your face," said Edmonton Oilers' Mike Krushelnyski. "If you were skating down low, bent over, it was like a sauna, the fog in your lungs. But if you straightened up, so your head was above it, it was like 'Ahhh, fresh air!'"

"I was very concerned that someone was going to lose an eye," said Wayne Gretzky. "The players who use white tape on their sticks, you couldn't see the blade of the stick. Mess (Mark Messier) said the same thing. You couldn't judge the puck, couldn't anticipate, because you didn't see it clearly. And it was hot. There were heat flashes all over the ice."

And when the fog wasn't enough, when the Oilers' Craig Simpson tipped Steve Smith's point shot past Boston goalie Andy Moog, tying Game Four of the Stanley Cup final 3-3 with 3:23 to go in the second period, the Garden hit the light switch and said: "That's enough." The building wasn't going to tolerate an Oilers sweep.

Flick. Darkness.

The police, and then the fire department, cleared the building. The fans were ushered out. The fog wouldn't go. The lights stayed out. *No más*, said the Garden. Get lost.

But out came NHL president John Ziegler. In person. He stood up on a box — the better for reporters to verify that it was really him, and not a cardboard cutout — and invoked Bylaw 27.12. Stating that the Garden had outsmarted itself.

The game would be replayed in its entirety, but at the *end* of the series, if necessary.

It won't be necessary.

Game Four moves to Edmonton now. The Oilers are 8-0 at home in the playoffs. You don't play in fog in Edmonton. The wiring is of this century. In Northlands Coliseum, as Jay Greenberg of the *Philadelphia Daily News* noted, the only acts of God that take place are those performed by Gretzky.

"I heard they were looking for Harry when it happened,"said Edmonton reserve defenceman Steve Dykstra. Harry Sinden, that is, the Bruins' general manager. But it wasn't Harry. The Bruins could lose $400,000 or more when they refund the tickets. This hurts.

"I don't know what's fair. I don't think anybody got robbed," said Gretzky, who — because the bylaw states that points scored in the nullified game still count — could end up with points in all five games of a four-game sweep. And it could turn out that Greg Hawgood's first-ever playoff goal happened in a game that didn't. It's safe to say there will be asterisks. Many asterisks.

"It was an unfortunate situation," Gretzky said, "but it was a tie game, and neither team should feel cheated."

The Bruins will, though, and maybe they should. They were tied 3-3, finally pushing the Oilers, and then their building let them down. Imagine: a 60-year-old edifice, with all that playoff experience, getting over-eager at a time like this.

Discipline. It's so important in the playoffs. The Boston Garden lost it. Couldn't stand the heat. Pulled the plug.

And so the Oilers, who wanted so badly to win this Stanley Cup on the road, may just have to settle for a victory lap around Northlands again.

Rats.

And fog. And lights out ... for the Bruins, anyway.

THE GREATEST TRADE OR THE GREAT CHARADE?

CAM COLE

August 10, 1988 — The Edmonton Journal

IT JUST WON'T stick: the image of Wayne Gretzky as the beaten-down, hen-pecked hubby, willing to give it all up for the girl. If it's true, I don't want to believe it. A lie would be better.

Anything would be better than the picture that emerged from Tuesday's standing-room-only press conference at Molson House, where Peter Pocklington handled the selling of Wayne Gretzky like he was delivering a eulogy. Which he was, in a way.

"It is with a heavy heart for our community and hockey club,..." he began one sentence.

"I don't believe in misleading the public,..." he started another. (A little honest laughter greeted that one.)

"Wayne Gretzky has given so much to our hockey club and to this city for the past decade, I believe he has earned the right to determine his own destiny,..." he said.

Sincerity dripped from every word. He never cracked a smile, and he even dabbed at his eye once or twice. I was moved. Truly.

"That (bleep) Pocklington," said the caller, a woman. *"Unfortunately, the sonsabitches got my money before they announced this. I will never, ever set foot in that building again, as long as I live."*

I looked over at Glen Sather about the time Pocklington got to the part where he credited Slats ("my best friend") with lending advice in making the deal, and saw the set of Sather's jaw, the murderous look in his eye. What was going on here?

"I'm from a small town," said a voice on the phone, *"and it's like a funeral here. How many games has Gretzky pulled out for the Oilers? Who's going to do that for them when he's gone?"*

Finally, Gretzky took the microphone.

He began to say that there comes a time ... but he couldn't make it. The sentence wouldn't come out, his face turned brilliant red, and he cried. He tried to compose himself, lost the battle and withdrew to a chair in the rear of the stage. Hung his head and wept.

"Calgary's laughing today," said the caller. *"They've sold the Oilers."*

Sather took the chair, and said that the Oilers will remain competitive — which is true — and that they might even win more Stanley Cups, but the job won't ever be so easy again — which is also true.

"Please, please tell me it isn't true," said the caller from the Northwest Territories.

There is no answer to that. All we can do is try to make sense of it.

The recurrent theme Tuesday was "Wayne wanted it." Pocklington said it. Gretzky backed him up. Slats nailed it down. Pocklington repeated it. "When Wayne approached me and asked me to be traded to Los Angeles ..."

It was like a performance, drilled and rehearsed — the start of the press conference was delayed more than half-an-hour while all the principals assembled their lines — and, in the end, flawlessly executed.

The operative word is executed.

Gretzky put up a brave front, but clearly he was despondent, and by Tuesday evening, we were beginning to suspect he may have had good reason. Paul Coffey said he spoke to Gretzky three weeks ago and Gretzky already knew the writing was on the wall. No suggestion there of "approaching" Pocklington.

Another Oiler, requesting anonymity, told a similar story of a depressed Gretzky, resigned to the fact that Pocklington was going to sell him — and the best he could hope for was to make sure it was to a city he could live in.

Gretzky, in L.A. Tuesday evening, said he must be the first player in history who was "forced to be sold twice in his career." What did that mean?

Here in Edmonton, though, Gretzky did his job. He bit the bullet, told the story the way it had to be told, and looked miserable.

But it was nothing compared to the anguish he left in his wake.

"This is the saddest day of my life," said an Oiler teammate, overcome by a sense of futility and frustration when it became apparent that No. 99 was gone. "How can Pocklington do it? Does he need the money that bad?"

It doesn't matter, really. Whether it's true or it isn't, The Franchise is gone. Gone to raise a family and save hockey in L.A. from killer apathy.

But he will never kiss a Stanley Cup again, or pose between the Art Ross and Hart Trophies. The battle is over. The rest is a rerun of Marcel Dionne playing out the string, finally succumbing to the indifference of the city, going with the flow.

And no more wrestling for the crown, either. The crown is Mario Lemieux's now, to have and to hold.

Wayne Gretzky lost all that Tuesday, and I can't believe he did it willingly.

"Well, if it's what Wayne wants, sure, we're going to be happy for him," said the man on television. *"But he's always been a Canadian and an Edmonton Oiler. He's an institution there — or was."*

The man on television was Walter Gretzky. And he didn't believe it, either.

JONES TAKES ON CAREER CHALLENGE

MICHAEL FARBER

August 10, 1988 — *The Gazette (Montreal)*

YOU LOVED HER in *The Flamingo Kid*. You cheered her in *Police Academy V*. You leered at her in the pages of *Playboy*.

Now watch Janet Jones as she takes on the most challenging role of her career.

Yoko Ono.

You remember Yoko Ono. Short woman. Plain. Could no more carry a tune than carry a piano on her back. John Lennon used to be a good singer before he met up with Yoko Ono. Lennon wrote songs everyone liked and was not appreciably weirder than your normal mega rock star. At least until Yoko horned in. Yoko manipulated him, snared him in her web. Lennon turned so namby-pamby, he even let Yoko sing back-up vocals.

Wayne Gretzky might not be in quite the same shape as Lennon this morning — cold, horizontal — but he is the next closest thing: Playing hockey in Los Angeles.

Jones, a B-movie actress from St. Louis by way of Hollywood, made the biggest trade in sports since the days Babe Ruth was a pitcher. Less than a month after she married Gretzky, Jones, who is pregnant, Yoko-ed her hubby to Hollywood.

JONES: "Wayne, let's blow this hick town and go to Hollywood."

GRETZKY: "OK, peaseblossom. But first, do you want to hold a love-in at the Queen E in Montreal?"

"If Janet moves back to St. Louis," Bob Plager, the Blues director of player development, said yesterday, "maybe we get him next."

Jimmy Carson, Martin Gélinas, first-round draft picks, a zillion dollars and 99 passes to the first Janet Jones Film Retrospective went to Edmonton in exchange for Gretzky and two manservants. In a way, the Oilers made out swell. If you think of a sports franchise as a living organism that must grow or die, Edmonton had a phenomenal growth spurt yesterday. The Oilers won a Stanley Cup without Paul Coffey, and in meeting Gretzky's and Yoko's fondest wish, Edmonton probably will win without Gretzky.

The body-for-body, statistic-for-statistic aspects of the Gretzky deal would seem to have a certain logic, but trading a national resource is beyond logic. Gretzky is as important to Canada as moose and mountains and Mounties, as important as the ice he skated on. You don't swap a natural resource for some nice, earnest young men who might score 60 goals.

Brazil had the right idea. When a European soccer team once made overtures towards the great Pele, the government declared him a national treasure. National treasures do not leave Brazil, which might be lousy at balancing the books but obviously has a keener sense of what is important than this pushover republic.

No, you can't blame only Yoko Janet.

This national disgrace goes right to the top, the head man, the league president. John Turner and Ed Broadbent have been bleating for a year about Prime Minister Brian Mulroney selling out Canada to the Americans; finally they have some legitimate ammunition.

Mulroney could have done something to stop the trade. Closed the borders. Grounded Air Canada. Asked Parliament to enact a Brazilian-style law that would declare Gretzky a heritage site. At the very least, he could have had customs officials change the forms so that in addition to rooted plants and more than $100,000 in cash or whatever, it would be illegal to import Los Angeles Kings hockey players.

And what of Peter Pocklington? The perfidious Peter Puck is rumoured to be a little strapped for cash, so he sells the Crown Jewel.

What next from that wacky province? Will Premier Don Getty call

Margaret Thatcher and say, "Listen Maggie, I know your country doesn't have any really great mountain ranges, eh, and it's been a lousy year for oil so maybe you guys could help us out by buying the Rocky Mountains. Whaddya say?"

The only way for Canada to redress this grievance is through the time-honoured process of — no, not of whining — legitimate protest. Boycott the United States. Cancel that motel room in Orchard Beach. Do not eat New York strip sirloin. And definitely refuse to watch any Hollywood movie, especially one that has a role that might be suitable for Yoko Janet.

Make the post-partum Yoko Janet look for another line of work, although come to think of it, she has had experience on the classical stage.

In the Great Gretzky Giveaway, she played Lady Macbeth.

CHAMPS GAVE ALL THEY HAD

ALLAN MAKI

May 26, 1989 — *The Calgary Herald*

MONTREAL — From the first days in Atlanta where fans didn't know a peach pit from a hockey puck, to the first game U.S. Olympic hero Jim Craig started in goal, to the time they found themselves in a new country, playing in a 6,000-seat closet called the Stampede Corral, who could have imagined anything as rich and rapturous as Thursday night?

The night the Stanley Cup came to Calgary. With Lanny McDonald scoring one of the goals. With Doug Gilmour scoring two of them. With Al MacInnis winning the Conn Smythe Trophy.

What an incredibly intoxicating evening. It was sweet enough to make champagne giggle. Al MacNeil, too.

In this showdown series against the warlords of Stanley Cup play, the Flames became the first visiting team to win the championship inside the fabled Montreal Forum. It marked the end of one era and the start of another. A big red era.

"To beat Montreal three games in a row, to be the first team to win the Stanley Cup here, what a feeling," said Flames general manager Cliff Fletcher. "There's no divine right in sports. You have to earn it."

The Flames earned this Cup. They sweated for it. Bled for it. Survived all the heartbreak a team could stand just to be a part of hockey history. In a dressing room packed with wives, friends and media, the images of this final were jammed together in a steamy celebration — Jiri Hrdina screaming in broken English, "Here we go. Here we go"; Sergei Priakin wearing a Stanley Cup champions baseball cap; and Lanny hugging his wife Ardell and looking like the happiest man to ever walk the earth.

"Lanny McDonald was one of the greatest things that ever happened to our hockey club," said Fletcher of those gaunt and early times, "because back in 1982-83 we were really a poor club fighting to get credibility. Lanny came in and gave us that credibility, so to see him score that goal tonight, carry that Cup around the ice, that to me was a fitting end to one of the greatest hockey careers a man has ever had."

The Flames were never really in trouble against Montreal on this fateful night. Colin Patterson turned a crazy hop into a breakaway score and McDonald's goal was right out of his highlight package of seven years ago. After that, the Canadiens pushed, but the Flames pushed back harder. Their determination born of a thousand setbacks and a hundred ulcers.

"This is a great win for the organization," said defenceman Brad McCrimmon. "I came here two years ago and in that time we've made about 12 (personnel) changes. We've just kept adding good players — Gilmour, Hunter, MacLellan and a bunch of guys I'm forgetting to mention. Everyone's come in here and fit into the puzzle. Everyone did his part. That's why we're champions."

And orchestrating this piece was the coach who only a year ago was feeling the pain of a playoff embarrassment in Edmonton. Terry Crisp became only the 12th man ever to play on a Stanley Cup-winning team and then earn another as a coach. The struggle looked as if it had taken every ounce of fight out of him. And his stomach.

"The difference (between the two Cup wins) is that instead of drowning 24 ulcers, as a player you drown only one. I think the turning point for us was winning Game Four, after losing that double-overtime game. The guys were focused. They focused their anger towards winning the Cup."

There was every reason for Calgary to falter; to knuckle under to Montreal's storied mystique. But the Flames simply did what they had to do to win. It was as if they felt, perhaps for the first time in their lives, that this was to be their special moment. No more last-second losses, no more questions about their lack of commitment. That era belonged to another team. The one Kent Nilsson used to play for.

"This was a long, gruelling playoff," said McCrimmon, whose battered nose was a testimony to just that. "It was close in every game with no room for error. Both teams were hustling and a bounce here and a bounce there could have changed things. All of us went through a lot to get here and now that we've made it there's no way to describe the feeling. It's unbelievable."

It was all of that in a rush of recollections and happiness. You could have seen them all on Lanny McDonald's face and in Cliff Fletcher's smile.

They had lived for the thought of this night. It was better than anything they had imagined.

FORMER FLAMES' COACH SUCCUMBS TO BRAIN TUMOUR

ERIC DUHATSCHEK

November 27, 1991 — *The Calgary Herald*

SOME OF THEM, the ones who played for Bob Johnson, wore make-shift black arm bands — hockey tape wrapped around the sleeves of their jerseys — during Tuesday's Calgary Flames practice.

"We wanted to pay tribute to him in some small way," said defenceman Gary Suter. "That's how he would want to be remembered — on the ice. He would have liked to have been out there, stickhandling with us."

Johnson, the winningest coach in Flames history, died Tuesday of an inoperable brain tumour at his home in Colorado Springs. He was 60. He had been in a coma for about a week.

Suter, who used to attend Johnson's hockey schools when he was growing up in Madison, Wisconsin, described his former coach as "a breath of fresh air at a level — professional sport — where you could sometimes be suffocated by negative things. He made it fun to come to the rink every day."

Johnson joined the Flames in 1982 following a successful 15-year coaching career at the University of Wisconsin and oversaw the development of the team from a middle-of-the-road club to a National Hockey League power.

Known for his enthusiasm and his ultra-positive attitude, Johnson took over a team that had posted its first — and only — losing record in Calgary. In four years, he led the Flames to their first-ever appearance in the Stanley

Cup finals, upsetting the heavily favoured Edmonton Oilers along the way.

"If you look back to '82 when Bob came on board, we were a team that was really in disarray," recalled former Flames GM Cliff Fletcher, the man who brought Johnson to Calgary. "We had a fledgling dynasty 180 miles up the road and Bob Johnson, in his five years here, made us extremely competitive.

"The one area in which he differed from most coaches is he felt there wasn't one hockey player on the team who couldn't improve, that even though they reached the NHL, they could become better hockey players. That sure was the case with us."

Johnson was the first U.S.-born coach of a Canadian NHL team. Flames defenceman Jamie Macoun first met Johnson back in 1982 when he was playing for Ohio State. Macoun, a free agent, flew up to St. Louis from Columbus, Ohio, to watch the Flames play.

"Afterwards, when I talked to him, the first thing that struck me was, here was this man, 50 some years old and he had the energy of a 16-year-old," said Macoun. "He was telling me this and telling me that and it was just non-stop for 40 minutes. He kept asking me questions and I never got to answer any because he was telling me what I needed to know anyway."

In his early years, Johnson employed many of the techniques he used in college. He would conclude each practice with an impromptu production that he called *Fancy Capers*, where a designated player would put on a spontaneous show for 30 seconds, which mainly involved some flopping around on the ice.

Johnson put a premium on fun, but he also stressed conditioning and the value of practice.

Soon after Macoun signed, Johnson used to make him push the nets from one end of the Stampede Corral to the other, wearing a heavy, leaded belt around his waist. Johnson wanted him to drop from 205 pounds to 195.

"He had me going up and down the Corral for literally 30 minutes with 40 pounds of lead on me," said Macoun. "I remember thinking to myself: I could be at school still, having a good time.

"But . . . when I think back on it now, all the little things he used to say made an impression. He used to compare things all the time. 'Do you think this is bad? You could be doing this or you could be doing that.' So no matter what happened, something — or someone — could be a lot worse off."

Johnson began his coaching career in 1956 at Warroad High School in Minnesota. He joined Colorado College in 1963 but made his name at Wisconsin where he established the hockey program in 1967 and turned it into an NCAA power. In 15 years at Wisconsin, he compiled a 367-175-23 record and led the Badgers to NCAA titles in 1973, 1977 and 1981. Johnson also coached the U.S. Olympic team in 1976 and was the Canada Cup head coach four different times between '81 and '91.

Johnson fell ill Aug. 28 during a dinner with his wife, Martha. He was rushed to hospital and originally diagnosed with stroke-like symptoms. Doctors removed one brain tumour, but found a second one and did not operate.

Johnson is survived by his wife, Martha, and five children — Mark, Peter, Sandi, Julie and Diane.

Diane, now 28, was born with cerebral palsy and has been institutionalized since she was seven at the State Home for the Mentally Retarded in Union Grove, Wisconsin.

"I don't get down about the little things," Johnson said last May, during the Pittsburgh Penguins' run to the Stanley Cup final. "I hear people, players, complaining, feeling sorry for themselves. They should have to spend a day in Union Grove. They wouldn't feel sorry for themselves anymore."

"He would always say: 'This is a great day for hockey,'" said defenceman Neil Sheehy. "Often, guys would ask: 'When isn't it a great day for hockey?' I guess today. Today is not a great day for hockey."

WHAT REALLY COUNTS:
A VISIT WITH TOE BLAKE

RED FISHER

December 18, 1991 — The Gazette (Montreal)

IT WAS COLD, the man on the car radio was saying. Snow, he added, was on the way later in the day. Five to 10 centimetres, maybe, so bundle up warm.

The snow that had fallen in the area several days earlier had formed soft, white pillows on the short driveway leading to the building. On the second floor, a white, lined face peered out of the window, and then quickly disappeared. "Chateau sur le Lac, Blvd. 16289 Gouin Ouest" read the sign in front of the two-storey building.

Toe Blake sat in a hallway wheelchair, his head on his chest, eyes closed. The top of the exercise suit he wore was as gray as the weather outside. The only small splash of colour on it was the CH. The words "Montreal Canadiens," also in red, were below it. The exercise suit bottoms were blue. His hands were crossed on his chest.

"Hi, Toe," said Floyd Curry. "Look who's here, Toe."

His eyes remained closed.

"Don't wake him, Floyd. He needs the rest," a guy said.

"Toe," said Curry, "we've brought you some cookies. Wake up, Toe."

A slim black man named Andrew placed a hand on Blake's shoulder and shook him gently.

"Wake up, Toe," he said. "Let's get you up. You've got visitors, Toe."

Then, he reached for the man who had been the very best of the National Hockey League's coaches for 13 uplifting seasons and shook him again. This time, Blake's eyes opened. An angry yell burst from his throat.

"That's it, Toe," said Andrew, his voice rising. "Let's get you out of this chair."

Almost two years have passed since Toe Blake was brought to this place. Only Andrew and the other warm souls who work there see him every day, talk to him, feed him and care for him, because they care. They smile a lot, talk a lot and, it's imagined, spread a lot of love around as only they can. They understand.

Andrew was on one side of Blake, holding and steering him into the bright, spacious dining room filled with empty tables. Curry, who once played on a Blake team, supported him carefully on the other side.

"There you go," said Andrew, easing Toe into a chair not far from the dining-room entrance. "There — isn't that good?

"Look what we have for you," he said, lifting a cookie toward Blake's mouth. "Eat, Toe, it's good."

Toe Blake, winner of eight Stanley Cups during his glorious seasons behind the Canadiens' bench, stared straight ahead, apparently hearing nothing, seeing less. It's what happens to people, Andrew whispered, when they're locked in the terrible vise that is Alzheimer's.

Or was he? Does anybody really know?

Once, everybody knew what Toe Blake stood for, how he felt, what he thought, liked, loved and hated. What he loved was to win. Losing was what he hated.

He was rough, gruff, intimidating, wise, compassionate, unforgiving, scheming and hard-working — all of it dedicated to winning his eight Stanley Cups as a coach, including a National Hockey League record, five in a row, in the last half of the '50s. Winning wasn't merely a worthwhile target; it was everything. It was life itself.

Blake wore his strengths as a coach on his sleeve: the dedication, the humour and the violent temper. That, and more — all of it tied in with a remarkable hockey mind.

Frank Mahovlich was one of Blake's greatest admirers. He felt Blake took care of 50 per cent of what was needed to win.

"I've always felt that a good coach is the one who wins," Blake once said. "But 50 per cent? If that had been the case with me, my teams would have won a lot more games."

Goaltender Gump Worsley once was asked what made Blake special as a coach.

"There are 20 guys in that dressing room," replied Worsley, "and it's seldom you find even two of them alike. He knew each individual — the ones who worked from the needles, the ones who needed another approach. Between periods, he never blasted an individual. He'd say some guys aren't pulling their weight. The guys who weren't knew who he was talking about and you'd see the heads drop. But he'd never embarrass anyone in front of everyone. His ability to handle players — I guess that's what you'd say made him great."

Was Toe thinking about Gump or Frank, sitting at the table yesterday, a plate of cookies in front of him? Once he was full of life and laughs and mischief and blessed with a thirst for winning. His eyes snapped and crackled with the joy of competition.

Now, at 79, his hair is white and his cheeks are sunken, but there was colour in them on this day.

"He looks good," said Curry quietly. "That's the best I've seen him lately. I was here a couple of weeks ago and he really looked terrible. I couldn't believe that was Toe."

Blake sat at the table, staring. He didn't open his mouth until Andrew gently brought a cookie up to it.

"It's good, Toe," he said.

"Eat, Toe, it's good," said Curry, who has devoted the last few years to taking care of the man who took such good care of Curry the player.

"Why wouldn't I?" asked Curry. "He was such a good guy."

Toe reached for a second cookie, then a third and a fourth. On and on.

"He wants something to drink now," said Andrew. He lifted a small glass of cranberry juice to his mouth.

Toe drew on the juice.

"*Merci*," he said.

Andrew looked through his gold-rimmed glasses and smiled. So did Curry.

"His appetite is fantastic," said Andrew. "He don't refuse food. He'll finish all of this. Most of the time, this is what he likes to do — eat. You haven't seen anything yet."

He placed an arm around Blake's shoulder.

"Does he watch hockey games on television?" Curry asked.

"Does he know what he's watching?" a guy asked.

"I would say yes, to a certain degree," said Andrew. "My belief is he knows. My own opinion is he knows."

Curry left to call to his wife, June. Toe — who always wore a fedora during his years behind the Canadiens' bench — reached for the brown one Curry had left on the table. In his left hand, he held what was left of the plate of cookies. With the other, he pulled the fedora toward him. Then, he ran his fingers over it — lovingly, almost. Then, again and again.

"He seems to like your hat," Curry was told when he returned to the table. "It's almost as if he remembers what a fedora meant to him."

Curry blinked quickly. "It's a damned shame, isn't it?" he said. "Look at his hands. He still has hands like a bear. Geez, he was strong. Look — he's finished the cookies."

Blake stared at the empty plate. Then he lifted it with both hands, tilted it toward him and let the crumbs fall into his open mouth.

"Good, eh, Toe?" said Curry. "Very good. Remember me, Toe?" he asked.

It is that time of the year — a time for breathing in deeply and reflecting on what really counts. A time for remembering the good times.

Remember Toe.

McSORLEY STICK CALL RECALLS CHERRY'S BLUNDER

MICHAEL FARBER

June 4, 1993 — The Gazette (Montreal)

THE CANADIENS WERE about to march to Death Row last night when, in a reversal worthy of Perry Mason, they threw the book — the rulebook — at the Los Angeles Kings.

Check the stick. Get away with murder. Eric Desjardins 3, Los Angeles Kings 2, in overtime.

The Christian 20-20 Excel model used by Marty McSorley will go down in Canadiens' lore right next to Don Cherry's first math book because he couldn't count to six in 1979. The illegal stick was the inanimate equivalent of Stan Jonathan, the extra man on the ice 14 years ago when Guy Lafleur sent the game into overtime and the Boston Bruins threw away a trip to the Stanley Cup finals in a Game Seven at the Forum.

Before we move into the bureau of weights and measures, it is worth remembering that the Bruins were two minutes from ending the Canadiens' string of Stanley Cups at three when Boston staged a Chinese fire drill on the ice. The Canadiens won in overtime, they went on to beat the New York Rangers in the final, and Grapes became a rich man. Sort of everyone won.

OK, so a Game Two isn't quite as immediate as all that, but for the Canadiens, it might as well have been Game Seven. There was an overpowering temptation in the third period when the score was 1-1 to say, "Next goal wins the Stanley Cup."

If Montreal had flown into Los Angeles today down 2-0, it would have been an almost impossible Lotus Land position from which to extract itself. The Canadiens had to take one on home ice, and when it came to crunch time, they had to lay on the lumber.

The Canadiens beat the murder rap on a technicality, as if referee Kerry Fraser had not read them their Miranda rights or something.

The stick call is not exactly the purist's way of winning a game. These used to be the Flying Frenchmen, not the Measuring Montrealers. But it certainly wasn't a cheap trick. Not at all. There is nothing cheap about the playoffs — not the ticket prices, not the price of a victory. If the red-white-blue needs to help to avoid the noose, it is time to turn to a little black and white. Rule 20B. After No. 28, Eric Desjardins, it was the absolute best number the Canadiens had going for them.

Guy Carbonneau spotted the stick. He says he noticed McSorley's out-sized curve in Game One. Captain Carbo is attentive to detail and no doubt has excellent vision. He might even have 20-20 foresight because McSorley said he received the batch of sticks he was using only yesterday.

Someone is not coming clean here.

But then, illegal sticks are hockey's dirty little secret. It's like cheating on taxes. You have known it done. During the Buffalo series, one of the Canadiens took a visitor on a walking tour of his own team's stick rack and observed "Legal, illegal, illegal ..." until he had eyeballed enough illicit wood to keep Fraser's already excited whistle in constant heat. This is how the game is played. The illegal stick is no different than the scuffball in baseball or holding in football.

As Denis Savard — one of the stick spotters who spent the night behind the bench — observed, "We're not talking about stuff that anyone goes to jail for. If you cheat, you have to be smart enough not to get caught. You cheat because you think it's going to make you a better player, and maybe Marty decided that stick made him a better player. I'm sure every team in this league has four or five guys who use illegal sticks. It's all a question of timing."

When to call it and when to change sticks.

Obviously, the Canadiens were going to wait until they had no choice because a stick call is the last call. It is desperate in the extreme, something done in the last two minutes. That explains why there is a flurry of exchanges with the equipment men in the last five minutes, which is like ditching the receipts before customs. Just in case.

Indeed, the Canadiens knew they had two sure choices for a stick measurement — McSorley and Luc Robitaille.

"Yeah," Carbonneau said, "until the other guy changed his stick with four minutes to go."

"Didn't happen," Robitaille said. "The only time I ever change my stick is when it's broken."

Sure. As if Robitaille is going to scream that all his sticks have a curve like Kathy Ireland and that he is always keeping one step ahead of the law.

Jacques Demers said he hated to do it to a player he respects like McSorley — he looked uh, terribly broken up about it — but the Canadiens were desperate, trailing 2-1 with 1:45 left in regulation. When asked if he would have tried the same gambit, Melrose said, "No, because I don't believe in winning that way."

Maybe Melrose didn't learn all that much when he played for Demers in Cincinnati.

"That's not a cheap call," managing director Serge Savard said. "That's an excellent decision by Jacques. You're not allowed to play with an illegal stick."

Did you ever?

"Me?" said Savard, the molasses defenceman. "Why would I ever have to?"

Savard was on the team that was saved by the Bruins' inability to learn the lessons of *Sesame Street*, and he stole another one because of an out-of-the-mainsteam penalty. His math is excellent. Instead of the Canadiens needing three games to get ahead, it only takes one.

The series is tied because Carbonneau didn't miss an old trick and McSorley did. It is part of the Canadiens lore, enough to make an outsider believe in spooks.

This was one for the books. Rule 20B.

ROY REIGNS AS BEST PLAYER OF THE SECOND SEASON

MICHAEL FARBER

June 8, 1993 — *The Gazette (Montreal)*

INGLEWOOD, Calif. — This had become Hockey Morning in Canada a good 20 minutes earlier, and there stood Patrick Roy. He had a mask, but he didn't have a cigarette.

He doesn't smoke. The Kings do. This was Stanley Cup overtime, that extra special place where the Canadiens have lived for the past seven weeks, but it was Los Angeles that was owning the extra time, throwing everything at Roy.

The Kings looked fresh. The Canadiens were like a punch-drunk fighter, searching out the clinches, hanging on, doing everything they could to fend off Kings. This was Rocky in Wayne's World, a tired team trying desperately not to get outclassed, and the only thing that was keeping the Canadiens alive was their goaltender.

"You know, I feel good in overtime," Roy said later. "I felt perfect. I just had to make myself tough to beat. You just don't want to give up a soft goal. My concentration came easy, especially in the third period and the overtime. I knew it would be a difference between 2-2 and 3-1."

John LeClair made sure the Canadiens are one win away from the Stanley Cup when he scored a 16-incher at 14:37 of overtime. Long John was Short John again, and his two game-winners put end-to-end would still be a gimme. But Montreal surely would have been back at its beachfront hotel if it weren't for Roy. He was Jacques Plante, Ken Dryden and Terry Sawchuck rolled into one. The next person he becomes is Conn Smythe.

Roy has been the best player in the post-season just as he was in 1986 when, as a rookie, he led Montreal to its last Stanley Cup. He is one Wednesday from a not-so-instant replay but in the overtime period, he surely turned the clock back to 1986 when he survived about a 3,465 shot overtime against the New York Rangers. Roy was called to stop a mere 10 in almost a quarter-of-an-hour against Los Angeles, but he was just as sharp.

When asked to compare the two, Roy said, "It's tough to compare this to 1986. We played so few overtime games then, and now we have one almost every night. But I don't live in the past."

Good idea. Why compare a Van Gogh to a Picasso? A playoff masterpiece is a playoff masterpiece.

"Patrick Roy is the greatest goaltender in the world," said Jacques Demers. "Kelly Hrudey (in the Kings nets) was great, battling, not giving an inch, but the Patrick Roy who came tonight was the Patrick Roy who is best in the game."

Roy made a reflex save on Jari Kurri in the overtime, a remarkable reaction as Kurri batted the puck in midair off Roy's glove. Of course, he couldn't stop what he couldn't see but then Roy didn't have to. His goal post did it for him.

Roy didn't have a clue on Jimmy Carson's shot from the faceoff in over-time. Carson was the bounciest player on the ice, Kings coach Barry Melrose having used him as sparingly as he uses the barber. That made Carson the most dangerous. He tried a cute play off a faceoff in the Montreal zone — Kirk Muller had scored on the same play in the first period when he took a faceoff through Jari Kurri's legs and shot it past Hrudey — and Carson got some serious stick on it. Clang! Roy still talks to his posts, and once again the post talked back.

"I wasn't thinking about overtime," Roy said. "I don't think our team was thinking about it either, not in a conscious way. But we know that when the score is tied and there are 10 minutes left in the third period, we're not going to take many chances. If we have a good chance, we're going to take it and go. But we're willing to go into the overtime."

Why not? The streak of overtime victories has reached 10 and the legend grows faster than the record for Team Time-and-a-Half, because now we're into exponents as well as opponents. The Canadiens now have won their past three games in overtime over the doubting Kings, the first final since Montreal-Toronto in 1951 to have a string of three overtime games. This was a little more lingering death than sudden death, but the Canadiens don't ask how long, they ask how much.

LeClair scored on a botched two-on-one on a play that should have been well past your bed time. But you probably stayed up and so did Roy, challenging the Kings to beat him. They couldn't when it counted.

This was no rout, but you better believe they are plotting a route, on St. Catherine Street this morning.

NEW MIRACLE ON ICE

JIM TAYLOR

May 1, 1994 — *The Province (Vancouver)*

IT WAS A series both teams deserved to win and neither deserved to lose. Sometimes they both made you wonder whether either deserved to be there. But they never did it at the same time, and in the end the only difference was that one goalie had more work to do and the other had a broken heart.

Maybe the *Hockey Night in Canada* people knew something, opening with the Eagles' *Heartache Tonight*. They just didn't know which way to dedicate it.

It turned out to be Mike Vernon, who beat a good and gritty winger named Stan Smyl in 1989, but this time was in against a different calibre Rocket. Without Kirk McLean, Pavel Bure would never have had the opportunity to fire, but somewhere in the local euphoria, raise a brew or two to Vernon, who must now face another summer of unfounded charges that he can't win the big one.

Vancouver 4, Calgary 3 — the third straight victory in overtime to win a series they trailed 3-1. The last time I saw a hat trick like that, its name was Paul Henderson. And let there be no late bandwagon-jumping on this one, by fans or media. If they'd held a vote on the Canucks' chances of advancing to Round Two, they'd have been wiped out faster than Brian Mulroney. We all knew they couldn't do it. We took turns throwing darts. If they ask us to be the dart board, all we can do is spreadeagle.

Lord knows, we gave them enough ammunition. McLean wasn't the goaltender he had been. Bure had polished up the disappearing act he pulled in the playoffs one year ago and now had it down pat. Geoff Courtnall had lost his scoring touch. Trevor Linden just wasn't playing like the Trevor Linden of the past.

OK, so Pat Quinn said when it was 3-1 that his team wasn't out of it. Three-Hat Pat? What did he know? Half the time (we never were big on fractions) he wasn't even there. Besides, he was too easy on the players. They'd tuned him out. Bring on Rick Ley. Bring on anybody. This team was in trouble.

Open mouth, insert foot.

Courtnall scored to win one. Bure scored twice to win the last one, including the big one in overtime. The other day it said here that McLean had to get back to looking more like Captain Kirk and less like Wesley Crusher. Last night, he looked like Jean-Luc Picard yelling, "Shields up!"

And then there was Trevor Linden.

Maybe he had lost a step in the latter part of the season. Maybe the self-installed yoke of being team captain slows him down from time to time. But when the Canucks drafted him they didn't just get a hockey player. They got a work ethic. And it has never been more apparent than in these last three games. He is not pretty to watch. There is no dance in him, no skipping around the rock. He just puts his shoulder into it until it moves.

They are crazy things, these playoffs. The Detroit Red Wings, the No. 1 team in the West, get blitzed by the San Jose Sharks, who snuck into the playoffs at No. 16 overall without much going for them but the title of Best NHL Team in California. The Pittsburgh Penguins are gone. So are the Stanley Cup champions from Montreal. They can rejig the playoff system till hell freezes over, but they'll never be able to hide the fact that hockey may start in October, but the real hockey begins in April.

Hockey fans know this. Every year, no matter which teams are in them, the playoffs leave fans muttering about so much dull hockey during the regular season, and why can't they play the league games the way they do in the playoffs. The answer is simple: Over seven games, a guy can crank up the intensity level. Try to sustain it over a stretch of 20 or 30 and your penalty box will have rubber walls.

For 1,092 games they mostly drive us nuts. A lot of the early playoff games aren't that much better. But the further they go, the better they get. And down at NHL headquarters, they laugh. They know damned well that games like this will make us forget.

GREAT END TO
A YEAR TO FORGET

ROY MacGREGOR

January 3, 1995 — *The Ottawa Citizen*

IT WAS A case of nature answering the call. It was the end of the worst year in the history of sports — a discouraging year when the main players wore suits instead of uniforms and all available statistics began with a dollar sign — but finally, mercifully, it was closing down.

A New Year, New Hope.

It had snowed toward the end of the worst year, but the snow had melted and hardened in patches. Right up until the end, the water remained open.

But then, on the very last day, a deep, bitter freeze descended. It fell over the open water and, overnight, four inches of solid, clear glass formed on the creek on the far side of the road.

Glass ice: something that happens only every few years — and it is not to be missed.

"The Eskimos," Margaret Atwood once wrote, "had 52 names for snow because it was important to them."

That figure has been much debated since she used it, but hockey players may have even more names for ice: new ice, old ice, bad ice, spring ice, choppy, rutted, scab, crystal, soft, hard, open, lake, slough, pond, creek, backyard, schoolyard, artificial, free ...

The best, however, is glass ice. It is rare and comes itself in two varieties. The first is what the Scots called verglas and is a fluke caused by a snowfall followed by rain followed immediately by a deep freeze.

In *The Game of Our Lives,* Peter Gzowski once described the day he and his boyhood friends came across this miracle in Galt: "The snow held again, and off we went, soaring across roads and frozen lawns ... 40 of us, 50 of us, gliding across farmers' fields, inventing new rules for our unending game, allowing for fences in the middle of a rush, or goals that might be half-a-mile apart. I didn't know if that had anything to do with hockey . . . but I know I'd never been happier."

The second variety is the glass ice that follows a hard, unexpected freeze when there has been no snow.

Someone noticed it when they were out walking the dog. They came back and got sticks and skates and neighbourhood kids and all set out for the walk out of the suburbs, across the road, past the farmhouse and down to the creek, where the rare ice was waiting.

The kids had never seen anything like it. They lay on their stomachs and stared down where the water was still moving over the gravel. A minnow darted, frightened by unexpected shadows.

Had the minnow looked up, it would have seen Canada.

It would have seen children racing and sliding and laughing. It would have seen long searches through the bullrushes for raised pucks. It would have heard a country's forgotten rhythm, wooden sticks on a puck.

Here was Long Pond, Nova Scotia, in the early 1800s, McGill in 1875, Queen's versus the Royal Military College in 1886. Here was the frozen pond, the river, the slough, the backyard. The Patricks and their wooden puck off Nuns Island, Maurice Richard on the Rivieres-des-Prairies, Walter Gretzky's backyard rink at 42 Varadi Ave., Brantford, Ontario, Bryan Trottier out on the Val Marie, Saskatchewan, slough with Rowdy playing goal, not a tooth left in the old dog's head.

At one point, where the creek and the glass ice stretched straightest from one twisting corner to the next, we held a hockey game. No corporate boxes, no tickets, no lockout, no doom, no gloom. We played for three hours until the kids could think of nothing to do but lie flat on the ice and stare down through the magic that may happen only once more in their childhoods.

"We shouldn't tell anyone," one of them said when we were walking home.

Oh yes, we should.

People in this country need to know, there is still a game out there, waiting.

MS. HOCKEY: IF GRETZKY WAS A WOMAN HIS NAME WOULD BE WICKENHEISER

ROY MacGREGOR

March 22, 1997 — *The Ottawa Citizen*

IT IS A story that, in time, may enter the sacred mythology of the game. They will tell of Hayley Wickenheiser's midnight skate as they tell the story of the neighbour dropping off a pair of old skates in the poor Floral, Saskatchewan, home where Gordie Howe was growing up.

It will become women's hockey's equivalent of Pierrette Lemieux packing snow onto her living room carpet in Montreal so her child, Mario, could play indoors, of Walter Gretzky taking his son, Wayne, out on to the backyard rink in Brantford, Ontario, and teaching him to carry a puck around Javex bottles, of Rejean Lafleur going into his son's bedroom in Thurso, Quebec, and finding 10-year-old Guy sleeping in his hockey gear, fully dressed for the weekend.

Hayley Wickenheiser's story takes place in Shaunavon, Saskatchewan, on a clear, cold December night in 1985. Tom and Marilyn Wickenheiser are lying in bed when they hear a mysterious noise. It is not the baby, Jane. They know it cannot be the four-year-old, Ross, nor seven-year-old Hayley, both of whom went to bed earlier, exhausted, from a long day of playing on the neighbour's rink.

Tom Wickenheiser hears the noise again. They have just had the kitchen redone, so perhaps it is just new wood settling. He gets up and goes downstairs:

nothing. He goes to the sink for a drink and stands there, staring out at the night. A clear sky, probably 20-below — and still only a little past midnight.

The sound again. He leans into the window, staring, and across the yard and across the alley, he sees something moving. A small shadow moving up and down the rink in the dark. And the sound again — of course: The sound of a puck on a stick.

"I knew there would only be one person who'd be out there," he laughs.

His seven-year-old daughter had been out for more than an hour. She had slept, wakened, and slipped out with her equipment after she knew her parents were asleep.

"It didn't matter about the light," Hayley Wickenheiser remembers, "I could feel the puck."

Perhaps no one in women's hockey feels it better these days. Only 18 years old, Hayley Wickenheiser is referred to as "the franchise" by officials in Canadian hockey. She is the inspiration for tomorrow's players; she is the hope for today.

If this country is going to emerge triumphant in the Women's Hockey World Championship that begins March 31 in Kitchener, much will depend on the way the puck feels on the stick of Hayley Wickenheiser.

"I'm very excited," she says.

And with good reason, for consider for a moment how Hayley's comet has shone: Most Valuable Player in the gold-medal game, 1991 Canada Winter Games, named to the national team while still a 15-year-old bantam, gold-medal winner in the 1994 World Championships in Lake Placid, New York, and earlier this month chosen player-of-the-game as she led the Edmonton Chimos to the national championship.

In theory, she could be 19 years old next year with two world championships and an Olympic gold medal to her credit — and still with her best playing days ahead of her.

The first-year general sciences student at the University of Alberta is one of the larger (5-8, 163 pounds) women in the game, but also one of the most skilled. A fine puck carrier with an excellent shot and extraordinary strength, she models herself on her childhood hero, NHL star Mark Messier, though she has often been referred to as "the Wayne Gretzky of women's hockey."

Messier — and to a lesser extent, Gretzky — became her role models when she was that seven-year-old in Shaunavon, and it never occurred to her that there was anything to prevent her from one day joining their team, the Edmonton Oilers, and playing alongside her male hockey heroes.

"I hadn't even heard of women's hockey until I was about 13," she says. "My aspirations were to make the NHL, just like any other kid. I was given that freedom to dream."

She was born at the right time and in the right place. It was no longer the 1950s when Abigail Hoffman had to become "Ab" Hoffman so she could play on boys' teams. The same year that Hayley Wickenheiser took her midnight skate, Justine Blainey won her Supreme Court of Canada decision to allow young women to play on competitive boys' teams if they had the skills.

Hayley Wickenheiser most certainly had the skills. Since she was barely able to walk, she had pestered her father, a science teacher, to let her play the game he played for fun and the neighbourhood kids seemed to play obsessively.

Shaunavon may have been a small town, but it was enlightened. Ken Billington and Jerry Mitchell were minor hockey coaches more than willing to welcome and encourage the youngster. Tom Wickenheiser also coached her, and her mother, Marilyn, became the team's chief fundraiser.

The other kids on the team, all boys, were glad to have her. "I don't think they treated me any different," she says. But, in fact, they did. She was, after all, the best player, the leader. "Really," she says. "I had to be, being a girl. It was easier that way."

The Wickenheisers are uncomfortable talking about it, but there were often scenes when the Shaunavon team travelled to other small towns. Parents would scream and swear from the stands; once three boys on an opposing team chased a frightened Hayley through the rink lobby.

"Sometimes parents have a difficult time if a girl scores four or five goals and beats their team," says Tom Wickenheiser.

It is a parent's tale Walter Gretzky would identify with. His own superstar child, Wayne, had to switch jackets with teammates before making the run from the visitors' dressing room to the parking lot.

"No one writes about how bitter parents are," Walter Gretzky once said. "I have been on both sides of the fence and the saddest part is they don't realize they have the best gift of all, a normal healthy boy. They are so busy resenting others who they think are better. They cannot accept that some boys are twice, three or four times as good as their son."

Or worse, that a girl could be twice, three or four times as good.

A few years ago, the family moved to Calgary so Marilyn could return to teaching and Hayley could find more competitive teams. She has played both women's and young men's hockey, though the games are dramatically different.

Women's hockey, she believes, is far more "European" in its approach, with much more passing and more emphasis on team play. Men's hockey, with its hitting, is far more physical, far more concerned with scoring goals. Two years ago she was a late cut from a superior midget male "AAA" team, but she still likes to play the male game because of its competitiveness.

"It's a different game," she says of women's hockey. "People are surprised at how fast it is. They can't believe how much passing we do. There's more to women's hockey than scoring. There's a respect out there."

Her own interest in the NHL game has diminished the more the league sinks into clutch-and-grab hockey and tedious trap defences. "It's not as exciting as it once was," she says. "I watch, but I sometimes get bored."

It is the opposite of what women's hockey is currently going through as national interest begins to rise around the world championships. Victory in women's hockey has become as much a matter of national pride as victory in men's hockey has always been, and the shift in public interest has had its effect on the life of the women's game's youngest star.

"There's been a shift in what people expect of me now," she says. "I notice a change in people."

It is also bringing change into her life. At the moment, she is a university student as well as a carded athlete, her income all of $800 a month. Hockey agents have called regularly over the past couple of years. There is talk of a women's professional league starting up sometime after the Olympics, and she admits to being very interested in the prospects.

Easton, the large hockey stick manufacturer, has contacted her about an endorsement contract.

"I'm just going along for the ride," she says. "All I ever want is to never have to buy a hockey stick again."

HOW ROME WAS BUILT IN SEVEN PAINFUL YEARS

ROY MacGREGOR

January 25, 1999 — *National Post*

BOSTON — Ho hum. Another easy win, another typical night's work, and the Ottawa Senators have defeated the Boston Bruins 3-1 to head into the All-Star Break in better shape than they have been since April 13, 1927, when the original Senators defeated the Bruins by the same 3-1 score to win their ninth, but possibly not final, Stanley Cup.

It has made them the darlings of the hometown fans and, it seems, everyone else's Second Favourite Team after the Habs, or the Leafs, or the Oilers. The team no one has yet learned to — or for that matter has had cause to — resent. The feel-good team of the 1998-99 NHL season.

The Senators are in second place in their division. Their captain, Alexei Yashin, is in fifth place in the scoring race and, this very night, on his way to Tampa for the 1999 All-Star Game. Their little goaltender — bespectacled Ron Tugnutt, looking more like a tired accountant than an NHL star — is leading the entire league in goals-against average. Once the new Airbus chartering them back to Ottawa lands, a cell-phone call to Tugnutt on his way to customs will inform him he is himself a late addition to the All-Star festivities in Tampa Bay. Well past midnight for a team that once used to skulk into and out of town, the Ottawa Senators will cheer the news as they stand in the immigration lineup, applauding customs agents adding to the welcome for the conquering heroes.

My, oh my, but how times have changed.

On the very first road trip of the new Ottawa Senators, in the fall of 1992 — back in the NHL after 58 years — the chugging turbo prop plane taking them to Boston had been forced to land in Hartford due to fog. The bus sent to fetch them arrived three hours late, and then the driver got lost on the way back to Boston.

In mid-March of that first season, back in Boston again and on the verge of setting an all-time record for futility — they still had yet to win a single game on the road — the Senators boarded another bus that was soon stuck fast in traffic. In desperation, they took to the subway, two dozen well-dressed young men with bags over their shoulders and sheepish grins on their faces.

A man with an enormous belly and a loud Boston accent happened to ask one of the young men standing beside him where he was from.

"Ottawa."

"Ottawa! Great city, lousy hockey team."

An awkward silence, then: "This is the hockey team."

Another awkward silence, then in full volume: "A hockey team riding da subway! No wonda you guys stink!"

And did they ever stink. *Sports Illustrated* would soon be calling them "the worst franchise in sports history." Everyone else called them "Road Kill."

They set that futility record — 38 road losses in a row — in Hartford on April 7, 1993, when the lowly Whalers scored four goals on their first four shots. Four days later, on Long Island, it was expected the streak would continue, only to have captain Laurie Boschman score an unexpected hat trick that gave the Senators a 5-3 win. At the bus, the players chanted "We Are Not Worthy!" as Boschman boarded a bus that, for the first and only time that year, would not be heading to the airport like a funeral cortège.

They had become hockey's equivalent to the 1961 New York Mets. The Senators might not have their opening day pitcher stuck in an elevator, or Casey Stengel claiming his top fielder was probably sitting in the centre-field stands, but they had their share of the wild and wonderful:

- At the 1992 expansion draft, they forgot to open the envelope containing the list of eligible players, causing them to select three players who were not available and leaving a national television audience with a lasting impression: "Ottawa apologizes."
- They wanted to pick a young Czech player, Roman Hamrlik, and build an ad campaign around the name 'Roman' and the Centurion logo — which Don Cherry had already described as a condom wrapper — and when they lost Hamrlik to Tampa Bay they fell back on an 18-year-old Russian named Alexei Yashin. They said they liked the way he played but they really liked the way he'd talked about the "environment'" during an interview.
- At the first-ever rookie camp, the *Ottawa Sun* sent a circulation manager, who had had a cup of coffee in the NHL back in the 1970s, to keep a daily diary. He ended up leading the camp in scoring.
- When thieves broke into the team's practice complex, they took the video equipment but left the game tapes. "Burglars with taste," assistant coach E.J. McGuire called them.
- In an ongoing battle to get permission to build a rink on the outskirts of Ottawa, the Coast Guard had to be brought in to prove that the stagnant trickle rolling through the abandoned corn field was not "navigable."
- Assistant coach Alain Vigneault was in such despair over the team's record that he took to running to forget his troubles. By Christmas he had dropped 30 pounds.
- The first-year Senators had only one highlight make ESPN's "Plays of the Year" when forward Andrew McBain got tossed out of a game in Chicago — and then promptly fell all the way down the stairs into the visitors' dressing room.

Well, what else could you expect? The Ottawa Senators had no right to exist in the first place. The whole scheme had been dreamed up by three recreational hockey players — Bruce Firestone, Randy Sexton and Cyril Leeder — over post-game beers in a tiny Ottawa arena. With Firestone providing the vision and the other two the *chutzpah*, they convinced a less-than-diligent NHL that they had the money for both the expansion fee ($50 million U.S.) and a brand-new rink. They came within a midnight fax of missing their first payments, and only survived after local entrepreneur

Rod Bryden came along and took over from Firestone.

They hired a general manager, Mel Bridgman, who had no experience and a coach, Rick Bowness, who had some, and together they set out to scramble through the first year. They made do with aging veterans like the proud Boschman and fan-favourite Brad Marsh. They added some bizarre rookies, like Czech veteran Tomas Jelinek, whose plastic skates squeaked and whose stick blades were so illegally curved, fans sitting back of the nets used to duck when he wound up.

The rest were castoffs or rookies, like Darren Rumble, who showed up for his road trip carrying sandwiches he'd made for himself and his own pillow. He had never heard of Air Miles.

"Wow!" Rumble exclaimed. "If they'd had 'Bus-o-Plan' when I was in the minors, I could go around the world for free!"

But somehow they won their first game, downing the mighty Montreal Canadiens 5-3 at the little Civic Centre and inspiring a headline writer at the *Ottawa Citizen* to wonder if "Maybe Rome Was Built In A Day."

But then the losses began piling up — 70 by year's end. The supposed silver lining in such disaster was to be the prize at the end, picking first in the 1993 draft, which meant a chance at the so-called "franchise player" of the day, Victoriaville's Alexandre Daigle. When it became clear that Daigle would go either to the Senators or the lowly San Jose Sharks, it began to be said that the teams were deliberately chasing last place. Bryden even went so far as to propose to the Sharks that the teams swap draft picks, thereby encouraging each team to do its best to come only second last, and thereby claim Daigle in the June draft. The Sharks refused.

In the final game of the year — once again against Boston — the Senators had to lose to claim Daigle on the basis of fewest wins.

They did, of course. And Bridgman was fired by Bryden first thing the following morning.

Oddly enough, halfway through the seventh season, the once-secret Master Plan of Randy Sexton and Mel Bridgman is no longer considered a joke in Ottawa hockey circles. Sexton had laid out a plan in which the team would stick with its young players no matter what the repercussions — including, it turned out, his own firing — and would, sometime between Year Seven and Year 12, challenge for the Stanley Cup.

That's pretty well exactly where the team is today.

Rod Bryden, who has recently raised his control of the team to 92 per cent, likes to say that his Senators are a rebuttal for that renowned Canadian — and profoundly Ottawan — attitude of naysaying all grand schemes.

People said they would never win a franchise, and they did.

People said they would never make their payments, and they did.

People said they would never ice a team, and they did.

People said they would never build a rink, and they did.

People said they would never stay, but they are still here.

People said they would never challenge for the Cup — but this story, remember, is still a long way from over.

THE KID, THE KARMA AND TIME

CAM COLE

April 17, 1999 — *National Post*

NEW YORK — The 9 a.m. plane to New York didn't have to leave Toronto's Pearson International Airport from Gate 99R on the day 99 retired. It just did. You could look it up.

I stared at the numbers as I waited to board, and grinned. Wayne Gretzky, believer in karma, would have enjoyed this. The forever frail-looking legend who turned a pair of matching digits into a signature, a guarantee of satisfaction that no one ever took back for a refund, went out yesterday in arithmetic symmetry, a man of his word.

The contract he signed at centre ice of Northlands Coliseum on Jan. 26, 1979, his 18th birthday, was a contract for his hockey life, as far as he knew, and it was to expire in '99. And as the final buzzer goes off, that's what the big clock reads.

Flanked by the commissioner, his family, New York Ranger brass, and two giant pictures — one, sober-faced, carrying the puck with the Rangers' new uniform on; the other, jubilant, raising the first Stanley Cup in Edmonton — the greatest hockey player who ever lived finally pronounced the words yesterday before a standing-room-only crowd in the Madison Square Garden theatre.

"I'm done," he said.

He wanted it to be a happy day. He had encouraged everyone around him to smile, be upbeat. John Muckler, his coach, couldn't manage it. On this rainy, maudlin afternoon in the Big Apple, he looked 70 years old.

"Yeah, I had a long conversation with Wayne," he would say later. "I don't think there's a career waiting for me in sales."

As Gretzky stickhandled around all the hard questions, it still seemed strange that a player so near to mythic stature in his own time should have called all four of the continent's major time zones home before he was done, growing ever more distant from the team and the city that defined him. Or was that vice versa?

But none of the scribbled quotes from yesterday's one-hour wake seems as powerful as the sense of loss now that it's official. It leapt from the television screen Thursday night in Ottawa more profoundly than it could have at a formal announcement a day later.

When his beautiful children cried — not understanding their mother's tears, overwhelmed by the outpouring of affection and the ear-splitting noise as Ottawa's generous fans let loose with their love for hockey's great Canadian statesman — who could keep his own tears from welling up? Not this cowboy.

"Well, there goes a pretty big part of our lives for the last 20 years," said my wife, Jan, who met him but once, at a team party after the 1988 Stanley Cup, the last he would ever win. She talks about that night still. She envies me the hundreds of Gretzky games I have covered, the hundreds of conversations.

I had never given the sum of them too much thought, myself, until this week. Because he would always be around, there would be much more to write.

But she is right. Though I've never been big on sports figures as heroes, at least not since I was old enough to understand how many of them would turn out to have feet of clay if you gave them half a chance, I was privileged to be able to see The Kid arrive as a 17-year-old with a teenager's complexion, able to watch him grow up in the Oiler dressing room, and able to try — and no doubt fail miserably — to chronicle and describe the wonder of 99, in all of his NHL uniforms.

And the 38-year-old who sat until the last question was asked Thursday in Ottawa, and then did it all over again while making it official yesterday in New York, never let us down.

It was an impossibly high standard, as much money as athletes are paid, as many ways as there are to put a foot down in the wrong place, as vigilant as the media is now. But he has always lived, and played, to a higher standard.

He was nervous, and faint of voice, as he began to reminisce. By question period, his younger son, Trevor, had fallen asleep. "Look at this guy, he's obviously really interested," Gretzky laughed.

The tape recorders rolled. Around the room, a few faces were lost in thought; people who had known him a long time ...

It's not, you understand, as though he was our friend. But there were a handful of writers around the league to whom Gretzky would extend an extraordinary courtesy, mostly Canadians, and to everyone else he was just damned decent — far beyond the norm.

It's not that he knew just how to knock off one-liners and sound bites to entertain the quick-quote grabbers. But he loved to sit around and talk about sports, to gossip, and joke, and tell stories and dissect games and peer into the future. He was, is, a real person.

You never got the feeling you were worshipping at his feet, exactly, but you would be jotting down notes and look up and all of a sudden realize you were part of a court, and he was holding it, and everyone in it felt included as equals, by his generosity of spirit.

One May in Detroit, sick as a dog with food poisoning, my teeth chattering, I fell asleep on the Oiler bus to Joe Louis Arena, a few hours before a playoff game. Gretzky, the last one off the bus, tried to wake me, saw I was in trouble, took me by the elbow and led me to a team doctor. The building was hot and I fell asleep again in the press box, waking only to the crowd's roar whenever a goal was scored.

"What happened?" I'd ask, and Frank Orr of the *Toronto Star* would say: "Kurri, 35-foot one-timer from the left circle, great setup by Gretz." I'd write it down and go back to sleep. In the room later, Gretzky asked me how I was feeling, did I get some pills, was I going to be OK, could I write? They had just won a playoff game. He was Wayne Gretzky. Where did all that humanity come from?

Why, from Walter and Phyllis, of course. From thinking, every time he was set to open his mouth: "What will Dad say when he reads this?"

There was a time in 1989, the spring after the trade, when the Oilers and

Kings were going to meet in the playoffs and I was summoned into a back room in the Great Western Forum, and there sat Gretzky. He was ready, finally, to talk about the hurt of the previous summer and his feelings about Glen Sather and Peter Pocklington, and for reasons I never understood, elected me as the messenger.

He recalled sitting in Kings owner Bruce McNall's office, with the telephone's speaker on, listening to McNall dicker with Pocklington over enforcer Marty McSorley, whom Gretzky wanted included in the deal. The Oiler owner didn't know Gretzky was in the room, but he had given McNall Gretzky's number and told him he was available — and now, Gretzky was making sure the deal was as good as possible.

"I couldn't give up McSorley without Glen's permission," Gretzky recalled Pocklington saying.

The Great One then hand-signalled McNall: keep pressing, he'll give in.

"Come on, Peter," said McNall, "you're not going to throw away $15 million (U.S.) over some frigging thug, are you?"

The deal was made.

Later that year, maybe early the next, Gretzky came to Edmonton when a bronze statue of him was being dedicated outside the Coliseum. He arrived in town, we met at a downtown health club, and for 90 minutes, he poured out his heart about leaving life in a fishbowl, where everybody knew everybody, to play in a city with a thousand celebrities. He was going to like living in the big city, he said. And he has.

We had our ups and downs, as columnists and sports figures will. The longest down lasted more than a year after I wrote a critical piece about his messy departure from the Kings to St. Louis. Gretzky, who reads everything written about him, took down the licence plate number and then — in one of his early games with the Blues — when I picked the Oilers' Kelly Buchberger as one of the three stars after he had elbowed Gretzky in the head and knocked him out, I was officially off the Christmas card list.

And then one day, enough time had passed, and as he walked with the Rangers to a practice in Edmonton, he made eye contact and said, "How are you, Cammy?" and extended a hand. My grandfather used to call me Cammy. No one else ever tried. But what could I say? The sun was out again . . .

By the time Nagano arrived, the end was near and everyone could sense it. His arrival with Team Canada on the bullet train from Tokyo had been like The Beatles in some chaotic scene from *A Hard Day's Night.*

I tried to position myself so that I could talk to him as he passed, in that madness, but perhaps 10 feet away from the cordon of cameramen and photographers in whose midst he inched toward the bus, I was picked up like a cork on the ocean, and carried along by thousands of closely compacted bodies, all screaming Gretzky's name. He looked at me, I looked at him. Recognition flashed in his eyes, then perhaps fear for everyone's safety, including his own — and finally amusement.

A week later, when the Canadians were out of the medals, and he had stood front and centre to answer for his team — even though he wasn't captain, even though he'd been passed over for the shootout — he was asked to do another stand-up with CBS. He looked down the long fence separating media from athletes, and saw me at the far end, hopelessly separated from the main group. It was early afternoon, but in Canada, newspaper deadlines were swiftly passing. He politely told CBS no, he had someone he had to talk to, and gave me five good minutes.

It's not as though we were friends. He just always has known right from wrong and decent from rude.

A part of me, yesterday, was glad that if he's going to remember Stanley Cups in his old age, he'll remember Edmonton and nowhere else. The other part, the sportswriter, wishes he could play forever and win it again.

The hockey memories are more of a blur, to be honest. I remember that I had to learn how to watch him play, at first, because his game was all understatement. He wasn't fast, but no one ever seemed to catch him from behind. He didn't have a great shot but he scored 92 goals one year. He was small, but trying to hit him was like trying to catch quicksilver in a butterfly net. He would do something you had never seen before, almost every game. But more often, he just appeared in a play, like an apparition.

And then, once or twice a game, the puck would seem to be attached to his stick with fishing line. It seemed ridiculous that the thing would follow him around for a whole shift sometimes, until you realized that he simply knew where it was going to be, and got there first.

The last time I saw a shift like that was at the All-Star Game in Tampa, Florida, a few months ago. He and Theo Fleury and Mark Recchi were all over the World Team's defence, buzzing the net — and in that moment, the years fell away and the grin on Gretzky's face as he came off the ice might have been from 1979.

Afterward, at the news conference to accept his All-Star MVP award, what he wanted to talk about was Rocket Richard, who had dropped the puck that afternoon. He wanted to make sure The Rocket knew how much he had meant to the game, and how lucky the NHL was to have had the fiery Hab as an exemplar.

Well, this generation had Wayne Gretzky. We were luckier still.

THE
GREAT ONES

JIM TAYLOR

April 19, 1999 — *The Calgary Sun*

NEW YORK — He walked to the rink this one last time with his dad, the way it was on so many nights and days and early mornings when the air snapped with cold and he and his world were young.

Wayne and Walter Gretzky, strolling from the posh Plaza Hotel to the storied pleasure palace of Madison Square Garden, not saying much, mostly thinking.

In the three years he'd been a New York Ranger, No. 99 had always taken the long way around to the dressing room, because that way he didn't have to pass the visitor's room and meet some of the players he'd be facing in a matter of hours.

But this time he led his dad through the regular door and walked around the building, looking at the walls and the pictures and up at the ceiling as though storing everything in the memory banks.

It was starting to sink in: After today, it really would be all over. Everything he did from then until the final horn, would be for the last time.

And then hockey would be over.

Later, he would tell the assembled media that "this is not a passing on, this is a moving on." And he'd be right, and they would come to see it. But this was late morning of the final game of his career, and he wanted his dad with him, the way it had been since Walter Gretzky sent a four-year-old wobbling onto the Nith River for his first stumbly strides to immortality.

He didn't know then that in ceremonies before the game, Walter Gretzky would skip introductions of the rest of the family, and reappear as the passenger in a new Mercedes-Benz, a gift from the Rangers.

He'd have laughed at the thought. One of them would say "Not like the Blue Goose, eh?" And somewhere in there, Walter would look at him and say for the 1,000th time over the past 32 years: "Long way from the river, Wayne. A long, long way ..."

He thinks he said it first on Nelson Skalbania's plane, when Nelson dictated the terms of a professional contract for a skinny 17-year-old who wrote it out himself on a piece of school foolscap because Wally was shaking too much to hold the pencil.

One plane flight, one decision, and his son's salary had jumped from $22 per game in junior "A" to a guaranteed $820,000 over the next four years. "Long way from the river," he said, looking out the window of the private jet. And, under his breath: "I sure hope we're doing the right thing ..."

And look at that car!

In Walter Gretzky's world — "A blue-collar guy who never made more than $35,000 a year but put it all into his family," Wayne told reporters — you weren't given cars. You saved, and you bought, and you ran them until they dropped.

Like the Blue Goose.

It was old and battered and the odometer had long since given up the ghost and settled on maximum, but it carried the Gretzky kids and members of their minor hockey teams to tournaments all over Ontario.

Wally drove, always. Late at night they'd be heading home to Brantford, and Brent would lean over and comb Wally's hair to help him stay awake.

One day he came home from work and there was a new car in the driveway wearing the Goose's plates.

"Phyllis!" he screamed as he barged into the living room. "Where's the Goose?"

"I got tired of telling you to sell it," she said, "so I sold it for scrap. The new car is from Wayne."

"Coulda got another 100 thousand miles out of her," Wally muttered.

But here he was, getting out of a Mercedes at centre ice at Madison Square Garden. And the White Tornado was a 38-year-old playing his last game.

Wally's eyes stung a little as he climbed to his seat and watched his son get one last assist, miss by inches a pass that might have given him a breakaway for the winner in the third, and wave a long and emotional good-bye to the Garden crowd.

He's back coaching, is Walter Gretzky. Not at 42 Varadi Avenue, though. The backyard rink he built every winter is a swimming pool now, a gift from Wayne and Janet the week 99 was traded to the Kings.

Little guys, like Wayne used to be. He is not too sure about the younger generation, these kids who call him "Wally" instead of "Coach," or "Mr. Gretzky," but they love the game, and that's all that matters.

On Saturday, I asked him how many NHL games he'd be watching now that his eldest son had said goodbye. He gave it some thought.

"Y'know, not many, I guess," he concluded. "It wouldn't be the same ..."

ROCKET ALWAYS MASTER OF HIS HOUSE

CHRISTIE BLATCHFORD

May 31, 2000 — *National Post*

MONTREAL — An honorable old saying here, born in the days when Jean Lesage was the Liberal premier of Quebec, was "*maîtres chez nous.*"

Its literal meaning is "masters in our house." But in the time of Lesage and Maurice Richard both, it meant so much more. French Quebecers chafed under the yoke of the English bosses who still ran the show; English was still the dominant working language; and when National Hockey League president Clarence Campbell suspended Richard for the last three games of the 1955 season and sparked the famous riot that is widely considered a turning point in Quebec history, the French had only small ways to show their fury.

"We all stopped buying Campbell's soup," Francis Lamarche remembered yesterday, at 65 able to grin now at the size and futility of the gesture. "All we would buy was Habitant soup; their sales went way up. It took years before we started buying Campbell's again."

In the most profound way, though he largely managed to remain an apolitical figure in the most acutely politicized part of the country, Rocket Richard was always the master of his house, by dint of his ruthless will to win and only secondarily his remarkable talent. His house was any hockey rink where he played, and yesterday, to the palatial new home of his only

NHL club, the Molson Centre in downtown Montreal, the people in their tens of thousands came calling.

By 5 p.m., officials of the Canadiens hockey club were estimating that 55,000 had already filed past his coffin.

Never has a hockey rink, let alone one in this part of the country, been so crowded and so quiet both. Never have the clichés of the game — that hockey is in Canada a religion; that the big, old arenas like Maple Leaf Gardens and the late, great Forum were shrines — held so true.

The crowds came into the building through the Windsor Court entrance, adjacent to the magnificent old train station of the same name. They were directed by black-clad ushers through a red-roped pathway that ran the length of the rink, past the wall of bronzes of the great Habs, past closed concession stands, to the far east end. Down 36 concrete stairs onto the bare arena floor, the people moved silently, filing through an area divided into lanes by more red ropes.

The Rocket lay on a bed of white satin.

He was not at centre ice, as has been described, but rather, as my *Post* colleague Jonathon Gatehouse noted, "in the slot, the high slot." Rather more fitting, Gatehouse said, for a man who set virtually every goal-scoring record imaginable, some of which lasted decades.

The Rocket's famously mad eyes, which had scared the wits out of NHL goaltenders as he bore in on them, were shut.

He wasn't wearing his Habs shirt, the No. 9 worn by so many of those who came to pay their respects, but rather a fine dark suit, white shirt and tie. His clever hands were still, folded on the great barrel chest.

At the sight of him, people knelt down or made the Sign of the Cross. Some touched the casket. Those who wore crosses around their necks touched them. Some blew kisses; one man waved goodbye. A few actually clutched their hearts. A great many wept openly at the sight of The Rocket; others held on until they had passed the coffin, passed his many relatives, who were gathered in a carpeted area behind the casket and had emerged into the bowels of the arena, where their faces collapsed.

Never were there fewer than about 700 people moving in silence on the floor of the rink. Never was anyone less than graceful. Not a single wrong note was struck.

Throughout the day, either The Rocket's baby brother, Henri, almost 15 years his junior, or his son, Normand, in a wheelchair because of a recent leg operation, positioned themselves to shake hands with the mourners. The two men stayed there for hours and hours, never too tired to thank people for coming, never too drained to murmur a few words; they made particular time for the disabled, the obviously disenfranchised, the elderly.

It could have been hokey, a caricature of a funeral service; it wasn't. The hockey club, with its collective respectful attention to detail, saw to that.

It could have been a circus, with great displays of grief from strangers and popping flashbulbs. It was not that, either.

The lone television crew in the place stood a good distance behind the coffin, and only a handful of photographers were allowed into the arena, far enough away from the crowds that they weren't noticed. This was no event for the media, but rather a throwback to the era when The Rocket was playing, when hockey fans mattered in a way they no longer do, when television was in its infancy, when the NHL allowed only the third period of a game to be broadcast, lest it affect attendance, when there were only two TV channels in Quebec, the mornings reserved for French-language programming, the afternoons for English.

Besides, all those who came seemed to have a personal connection to The Rocket; they all felt they did, anyway.

Lamarche, of the Campbell's soup story, won $500 in a hockey pool because of The Rocket, who scored the last goal of a game at 12:18 of the third, giving Lamarche a $500 win. "I remember I went to my sister's house with the money," he said. "I had $100 in dollar bills and I came in and just threw the bills at her kids."

Lamarche's friend, 67-year-old Georges Dube, clutched a glossy souvenir book about The Rocket in which, to his delight, he discovered a picture of himself at 22, holding a papier-mâché head of The Rocket and waving an anti-Clarence Campbell sign with a pig on it. There were three of them together that night, Dube said, in a white pickup, and they drove around and around the old Forum in a "peaceful demonstration" before the police sent them home. Later, in the first period, with Detroit leading 4-1, someone threw a stink bomb, and the infamous riot unfolded in the streets. Dube stayed home.

"I feel I lost a friend," Mr. Dube said. "He was that close to the people." When he filed by The Rocket's coffin, he wept like a baby.

First through the doors of the arena yesterday were three non-Quebecers, 20-year-old Grant Karn and his retired schoolteacher dad, Bob, from the little town of Rodney, near London, Ontario, and 53-year-old Fred Douglas of Milton, Ontario.

The Karns drove here Sunday night for two reasons, Grant said. "One is for him," he said, gesturing to his dad. "One is for me. My father grew up listening to Maurice Richard on the radio, and I grew up listening to my dad talk about him."

Douglas was in town on business and came to the Molson Centre at dawn. "I played millions of games in my basement, against the wall," he said, imagining himself as Maurice Richard. In those days, he said, "in music, it was Elvis. In hockey, it was The Rocket."

Standing with them was André Malouf, who is now 57 and who first went to the Forum in 1948 as a child of six with his father. Malouf was decked out in his Habs jacket, shirt and hat. He's a professional psychic, but, he said, he didn't really see The Rocket's death coming. "In my mind, he wasn't finished the work," he said.

That work had honour.

It was, though never put so crassly, to remind the first nation of hockey of the goodness of the game, of the way it could make a man a hero almost against his wishes, of the unifying force it can be. The Rocket was a formidable figure on the ice, but intensely private off it. His brother, Henri, told *La Presse* this week that he guessed all the conversations he ever had with his big brother would have amounted to no more than a half-hour on a cassette tape.

Bert Raymond, the great sportswriter for *Le Journal de Montreal*, sat by himself in a corner of the stands at the Molson Centre yesterday, watching Henri Richard, impeccably dressed in sports jacket and tie and looking still every inch the great athlete he was, greeting hundreds of mourners. "Look at him," Raymond said. "He's 64 and he's still shy." And he is, but as his more famous brother did so often, on and off the ice, The Pocket Rocket was rising to the occasion, speaking the best and most enduring language of this immense country, remembering the time when Canadians were, indisputably, masters of their hockey house.

THE LION
IN WINTER

ROY MacGREGOR

March 24, 2001 — *National Post*

EAST RUTHERFORD, N.J. — Here, on another spring day seven years ago, the Legend of Mark Messier was born. It was, just as it is this night, a game between Messier's New York Rangers and the New Jersey Devils. Unlike this night, however, that other game counted for something: the Rangers were on the brink of playoff defeat and Messier, the Rangers captain, not only "guaranteed" victory but went out and, virtually single-handedly, beat the Devils by scoring a dramatic hat trick that included the tying goal and the winner.

It allowed the Rangers to move on and eventually claim their first Stanley Cup in 54 years. Messier was then the toast of the city: dates with Madonna, guest of Letterman. The nickname he'd carried through five Stanley Cup wins in Edmonton — where his "brilliance," *The Washington Post* archly stated, had gone "unnoticed in the vast Canadian Prairie" — took on new meaning. "Mess" became short for "Messiah."

Seven years is a generation in professional sports. He is 40 now, once again back in New York City as captain of the Rangers, but the team is neither defending the Stanley Cup nor challenging for it. The media that once lionized him has, at one point this season, asked, "How do you tell a living legend he is dead on his feet?" Ranger fans who cheered in the streets seven years ago have come to this game with paper bags over their heads.

The Devils, instead, are the reigning Stanley Cup champions, and this night will extend a late-season winning streak to an even dozen. In a 4-0 loss, the Rangers will count only 11 shots, none of them by Messier.

And yet, when it is over, Rangers coach Ron Low will say that Messier and Radek Dvorak, his 24-year-old linemate, were the only two forwards who even tried this night. When Messier himself meets the media throng, he casts no stones, saying he failed to get things going, as is his job.

No one dares ask about the more recent "guarantee" Messier made — that this year, with him back, the Rangers would make the playoffs after a three-year drought.

"If they don't make it," says Martin Brodeur, who was in goal for both Messier's 1994 hat trick and tonight's shutout, "who's going to mention it to him? Tell me that."

Earlier this week, there was a surprising bump in the National Hockey League record book: Mark Messier, who scored only one goal in his first 52 games as a professional, pushed aside Marcel Dionne and moved into the No. 3 position in all-time scoring, behind only Wayne Gretzky and Gordie Howe.

Once Howe's 1,850 points had seemed unassailable; then came Gretzky to score 2,857; now Messier stands just 77 points back of Howe. At Messier's current rate of scoring — .819 points per game, his highest in four seasons — he might do it by the end of next season, or the beginning of the following.

"It's a funny thing," says Scott Stevens, the Devils captain, "but when you think of Mark Messier you don't think of points."

Players think, instead, of The Stare, the look, the menacing glare that, in a face-off circle, is not unlike that of Ted Williams in the batters' box or Sonny Liston in the ring. This, after all, is the player who, during his career with the Edmonton Oilers, once threatened to toss griping Jimmy Carson out of a plane 30,000 feet over the Prairies.

When the big, 15-year-old kid first tried out for his father's Tier II junior team in St. Albert, Alberta, he came across a roster sheet on the dining room table with three big question marks scrawled beside his name. He figured if he had any future at all in hockey, it would be as an enforcer.

"I was always a little younger playing against older kids, always moving up," remembers Messier. "I never had any opportunity to excel. I was never the top goal scorer or the star. I had to develop at the pro level — and I was slow to do that."

He was, however, big and tough, the skills hockey sought in the 1970s. When he was only 17 his Tier II coach and father, Doug Messier — who had himself been a minor-league professional — figured the boy "was ready for more." He put a call in to an old defence partner, Pat Stapleton, who was then coaching the World Hockey Association's Indianapolis Racers, a shaky team that had just lost its only star, another 17-year-old named Wayne Gretzky, to the Edmonton Oilers.

Stapleton agreed to take him on, but the franchise itself survived only five more games. Messier caught on with another weak WHA team, the Cincinnati Stingers, scored his first pro goal on a high flipper from centre, and soon enough that team was also history and he was off to join Gretzky in Edmonton, with the Oilers now part of the NHL.

He developed slowly. He always had speed, but also a temper, and it took time for him to show what Peter Gzowski would later call that "controlled fury" on the ice that others would find so intimidating. He became a shooter and a playmaker and soon was an all-star, a five-time Stanley Cup winner and twice the league's Most Valuable Player.

When the Oilers could no longer afford their stars, he eventually followed Gretzky to the rich U.S. markets, taking up in New York where he brought them the Stanley Cup and they gave him a three-year deal for $25 million U.S. No longer was he going "unnoticed in the vast Canadian Prairie."

It is hard to place a date on it, but at some point in recent years some people began to look differently at Mark Messier. After Canada's loss in the 1996 World Cup, a movement began "to turn the page" in Canadian hockey. His six Cups, his victories in the Canada Cups and his reputation for leadership counted for nothing when they put together the entry for the 1998 Winter Games. Gretzky, too, might have been left off if organizers had the nerve. There was some public outcry at Messier's absence, but on one level it seemed to make limited sense. There was a symbolic torch to pass on — this time to young Philadelphia Flyers captain Eric Lindros — and while Gretzky seemed comfortable with inevitable change, no one doubted that Messier would have assumed the leadership whether or not he had the captain's "C." His personality was that strong.

"It was a huge blunder," says Messier's current coach, Ron Low. "It doesn't make any sense to mock those who were in the system then, but to leave one of the greatest leaders in the history of sports off the hockey club?..."

Messier knew that his old friend Gretzky, now leader of the Canadian entry in the 2002 Olympics, would be naming his first eight players this week. He also knew his name was not up for consideration. Nor does he expect to be one of the 15 to be named later, though some would say his overwhelming will to win is exactly what was needed in Nagano.

"They're going to be criticized for whoever they pick," he says. "But I've had a pretty good run. I have no complaints."

He has had to grow used to hearing those of others, though.

Messier started wonderfully, faded, and is again playing well. He has suffered silently through the pitiful seasons of his usual linemates, Adam Graves and Valeri Kamensky. He has, because of injuries, played with wingers who came up and were soon sent back to the minors. His best hockey of the year has been over the past couple of weeks as he has played with two youngsters young enough to be his children in Dvorak and Manny Malhotra.

"It's an honour to be on his wing," says the 20-year-old Malhotra, who remembers playing street hockey in Mississauga, Ontario, and kids fighting over who would be Messier. "He's so focused, you can't help but be affected by it."

There was a time this year, however, when the famous focus slipped. During a 14-game stretch that effectively put an end to the Rangers' playoff hopes, Messier hit a psychological bottom. "He was down," says Low, "I mean very down. I talked to him and I told him: 'Look, you can't take it all on.' But it's automatic with him. He said: 'Yeah, well it's my job to make everybody around me better.' I said: 'Well, there are certain times when it ain't happening.' But that's the way he is."

Doug Messier, who is also his son's agent, says he tried to talk to Mark about it, but couldn't get through to him. "He takes on too much," Doug Messier says. "He's always been that way."

The winning, he now says, will begin next year. Guaranteed.

But next year, he will also be 41. Increasingly, it will be that statistic they refer to as much as whatever gap remains between him and Gordie Howe's once-unreachable record. When he hit 40 he told the media that "it doesn't mean one single thing to me." He keeps himself in remarkable condition — and, besides, Gordie Howe retired at 52.

NO REGRETS: THE CANADIAN HOCKEY TEAM BOSS SAYS HE SPOKE OUT, LOUDLY, TO 'PROTECT' HIS PLAYERS

WAYNE SCANLAN

February 20, 2002 — *The Ottawa Citizen*

SALT LAKE CITY — He was much quieter as a player, Wayne Gretzky. Spent 20 years carving out a polished, public persona as a dull figure. The veins in his neck didn't bulge, his teeth didn't grind. He never looked like the guy on his way home to kick the dog and yell at the kids.

And in one night, Gretzky turns into the maple leaf version of Rush Limbaugh.

In his now famous "Canadian Rant," Gretzky has people wondering what happened to the guy who played hockey so brilliantly, then talked so sparingly.

Reaction the world over seems to be split. Many Canadians are happy to see The Great One stand up and speak out with the kind of passion his team has lacked until Monday night's 3-3 tie with the Czech Republic. Others wonder what caused this sporting icon, a man who is part of Johann Olav Koss's Olympic Aid program for disadvantaged children in Asia and Africa, to suddenly speak of the need for Canadian players to learn to hate their international opponents as much as they hate us.

Hate, in the sporting, arch-rival sense, of course, not the real kind that has countries at war.

Yesterday, for his contributions to the game of hockey, Gretzky was awarded the highest honour of the Olympic movement, the IOC's Olympic Order.

The night before, Gretzky was ordering up an on-ice payback against Czech player, Roman Hamrlik, for a cross-check on Canadian forward Theo Fleury.

"Maybe my timing was not good on that one," said Gretzky, laughing, at the juxtaposition of the award and his tirade. He explained that he spoke out to "protect" his team, which has a win, loss and tie heading into today's quarterfinal against Finland.

"Every day when I came to the rink, there was another rumour ... the coaches weren't talking and Mario (Lemieux) was going home. Finally, I'd had enough of it."

The rumour about his captain, Lemieux, leaving the Games because his hip was too injured to play, was the "last straw," said Gretzky. He had, he said, no regrets about his outburst, though the line about Canada being victim to "American propaganda" was in jest.

"My kids asked me what propaganda was," said Gretzky. "I said, I don't know. I just said it."

On Monday, Gretzky stepped out of his icon mould in a big way, working himself into an emotional lather, suggesting the world has it in for Canadian hockey, that some television coverage of Canada's team here sickened his stomach.

In a separate press conference in the E Center arena yesterday, one American journalist asked NHL commissioner Gary Bettman how he felt about Gretzky "propagating hate."

Bettman's response was that he believes Gretzky was propagating "passion."

It isn't easy to imagine Gretzky as a controversial figure, his comments posted in dressing rooms and shared feverishly by reporters. When Gretzky, the player, spoke, it was almost always with the soft tones and diplomatic mantra of hockey's foremost ambassador.

Under the most excruciating pressure and difficult circumstances, Gretzky never lost his grace and dignity. He avoided controversy as though it were a flu virus.

In Nagano, at the 1998 Olympics, his international farewell as a player, Gretzky didn't flinch or whine about playing a bit part, like a Hollywood movie extra, in Canada's bid for the gold medal. He refused to complain when he wasn't included in the infamous shootout lineup versus Dominik

Hasek and the Czech Republic in the Olympic semifinal. Media and hockey fans complained on his behalf. They still do.

This new Gretzky, the one who had a public meltdown following Monday's game with the Czechs, is Gretzky the Suit dealing with the stress of being the lead man on Canada's bid to end a 50-year gold-medal drought in Olympic hockey.

These Olympic matches are killing Gretzky. He views them like a goaltender's mother, fearful and fully stressed. A sportswriter from Winnipeg said that "if the Canadian team played half as hard as Gretzky watched the games, they'd win easily." Gretzky admits it's a "different feeling," more anguishing than as a player. "Brett Hull (of Team USA) told me he's enjoying watching me (worry) on TV more than anything else."

As for the theory that Gretzky was trying to provide a Glen Sather-like distraction, the kind used by his former Edmonton Oilers coach, Gretzky denied it.

"Was it staged?" said Canadian Hockey Association president Bob Nicholson. "Absolutely not. It was how he felt. You've seen Wayne Gretzky the player and the executive director — now you're seeing the hard-core GM."

Sounding like an ordinary angry man, maybe an NHL goon or WWF wrestler, Gretzky threatened that Roman Hamrlik, would get his "payback" when Hamrlik's New York Islanders face Fleury's New York Rangers in an NHL game next week.

It was the kind of raw, emotional comment that a hockey coach might make in the heat of the moment after a tough game. Gretzky's rant will be talked about from now until the medal presentations, and then some. He has his hands all over this Team Canada entry. He speaks like a coach, frets like a GM and burns to win with the passion of the fiercest Canadian hockey fan.

There's something about the international arena that brings out the best and worst of Canadian hockey figures.

Who can forget Team Canada czar Al Eagleson being hauled across the ice in Moscow in 1972, days after captain Phil Esposito passionately scolded Canadian fans for falling off the bandwagon?

And there's something about these Olympics that continues to find Canada in the middle of a storm.

"The Canadians used to be known as the quiet ones of North America," *USA Today* wrote the other day, following the raging controversy over Canadian figure skaters Jamie Salé and David Pelletier.

"Now, you can't get them to stop talking."

Skategate gives way to Wayne's World.

With luck, the hockey games and not the gabfest will be the story from now to Sunday.

GOLDEN REDEMPTION FOR CANADA'S WOMEN

ALLAN MAKI

February 22, 2002 — *The Globe and Mail*

WEST VALLEY CITY, Utah — For more than a week, they bore their opponent's taunts with smiles and silence. They talked instead about how much they respected the U.S. women's Olympic hockey team. They said nothing about the little things that were being done to irritate and belittle them; little things such as having their photographs at the athletes' village scribbled on and autographed by the American players.

And the business about the Canadian flag. Did it really happen? Did the Americans have a Canadian flag in their dressing room? Was it sneered at and mocked as a symbol of weakness?

The Canadians heard it was so but stayed calm. Redemption would be theirs. Redemption for the eight-game losing streak they had endured before these Olympics, making the U.S. everyone's pick to win gold in Salt Lake. And redemption, to be sure, for the gold-medal game the Canadians had lost four years ago in Nagano.

They got it last night with a 3-2 win that had Canada's best female hockey players standing together, arm in arm, crying tears of joy instead of frustration. They got it by overcoming a partisan crowd, an inordinate number of American power plays (11) and a team that had gone 35 games in a row without losing a game, until last night.

And what a night it was for Canada. Its women's team scored early and late. Simply put, the players refused to lose. They didn't want to endure the agony of Nagano, when they stood on the blue line at the end of the game and watched the Americans accept the gold medals Canada had been expected to receive.

"The worst part was hearing their national anthem," recalled assistant captain Vicky Sunohara. "There was no way we wanted to hear that again tonight."

They had already heard and seen enough leading up to the final. According to several Canadians, the U.S. players helped cook their own goose through their off-ice foolishness.

Sunohara said that there were "certain acts of disrespect" thrown at the Canadians. She talked about the photographs of Lori Dupuis and Kelly Bechard that were drawn over and written on by the American players who happily left their names.

"We took the photographs and put them in our dressing room," said Sunohara, who was told a Canadian flag had been hung in the U.S. room. "I don't know what was being done with it. We heard a lot of different things that were said about us. We didn't say a thing back. We were down 0-8 to them. We said, 'Let's do it when it counts' and we did. Maybe we should thank them. It fueled the fire. It gave us motivation."

The Canadians took a 1-0 lead on the U.S. then countered with a goaltender, Kim St-Pierre, and a penalty-killing unit that was overworked but seldom better. That Kelly Livingston, an American, was allowed to referee such a crucial game made her every call open to interpretation, and the fact she called so many penalties in favour of the U.S. only hardened the Canadians' resolve to be stronger, tougher.

"We showed true character. I looked in their eyes and I saw fear," said Hayley Wickenheiser, whose second-period goal came soon after the Americans' first and put Canada back on top 2-1.

"Hayley Wickenheiser's a great hockey player but maybe she's not an optometrist," countered U.S. coach Ben Smith.

If you watched last night's final, you saw a game with drama and tension and all types of story lines. Inside and outside, the E Center was crackling with emotion. Outside, scalpers were asking for as much as $600 U.S. for a single ticket and getting it. Inside, there were signs and banners and flags everywhere, including one for each country on the two Zambonis, which were driven by women, a nice touch for the evening's event.

As the Canadians had hoped, their goal at 1:45 of the first period rattled the U.S. and turned up the pressure. Patrick Roy may not be playing for Canada at these Olympics but one of his biggest fans, St-Pierre, did a pretty mean imitation. In the second period, her sprawling glove save tipped the puck just enough to send it off one of the posts behind her and out of harm's way. From then on, the Americans were flustered and nervous.

"I can't believe it," said St-Pierre, who led Canada to last year's world championship, its seventh in a row. "This is what I've dreamed of, to be here with a gold medal. Our team played so well."

Every player on the Canadian roster had the game of her life. They were hungry and spirited but always in control. And when it ended, and they stood on the blue line and looked at the Americans with their silver medals, they thought of Nagano and smiled.

"Some people said, 'If you don't come home with the gold, don't come home,'" Danielle Goyette said with a laugh. "Now we can come home, and we have the gold medal."

It looked awfully good on them. It gave them the respect they so dearly wanted and now deserve. Call it a 24-karat payback.

GOLD RUSH, EH? HOCKEY VICTORY CROWNING ACHIEVEMENT OF OLYMPIC EFFORT

DAMIEN COX

February 25, 2002 — *The Toronto Star*

WEST VALLEY CITY, Utah — We know now that our loonie is worth far more south of the border when it's covered by a thin layer of ice. In that form, at the right moment, it can buy 23 pieces of gold and a perch back atop the hockey world.

The crowning moment of Canada's most successful venture ever into the Olympics of snow and ice came yesterday with the country's first set of gold medals in men's hockey in 50 years.

To the 1952 Edmonton Mercurys, Canada can only apologize for taking so long to follow up on their accomplishments. It took 11 tries, including three silver finishes and two bronze medals, but the Mercs finally have some new company in Canadian hockey history.

Yesterday's rousing 5-2 triumph — a numeric coincidence? — over the previously unbeaten host Americans on the final day of the 19th Winter Olympics happened with a Canadian loonie secretly buried under centre ice by a mischievous crew of ice-makers, most of whom had been imported from various parts of Canada.

"It was a cool idea," said Team Canada executive director Wayne Gretzky after digging the dollar coin in question out of his pocket. "It's going to be a great thing to have in the Hall of Fame.

"I'm happy for the Canadian people. They waited a long time for this. We desperately needed to win this tournament."

Canada's seventh gold medal in the history of the Olympic men's hockey tournament came on the heels of the gold-medal triumph of the women's team two days earlier, which also came at the expense of the United States.

"(Hockey) might be the only game they're good at," said a half-joking U.S. captain Chris Chelios.

Not true, sir. But from hockey to speed skating to figure skating to the crazy short-track stuff, these certainly were the Games of the flashing skate blade for Canada, as Catriona LeMay Doan and Marc Gagnon and Mario Lemieux combined to prove that we might have some eccentricities as a country, but we sure can skate.

Forget those official medal standings, Canadian athletes will be taking home a total of 77 medals. That's 55 gold, seven silver and 15 bronze. There are 46 gold medals coming back here from the twin hockey victories alone.

This hockey team, the result of Gretzky's imagination, survived a dreadful start to the tournament, a 5-2 loss to Sweden, and by the final days had congealed into an impressive squad that achieved a remarkable level of understanding between players in such a short time.

As Canadians celebrated, the entire Team Canada organization seemed to understand instinctively the enormity of what it had accomplished.

"It was a chance of a lifetime to be here," said Lemieux, who came out of retirement last season with the expressed desire to play for Canada in Salt Lake City. "Having the chance to do something like this for your country is awesome."

With Canada safely ahead by three goals, thousands of Canadian fans began an impromptu rendition of O Canada — with 40 seconds left — that grew louder and louder, a spontaneous outpouring of joyful patriotism that sent shivers down the spines of more than a few Canadians, including the players.

"It was a great feeling to be on the bench and hear that," said winger Brendan Shanahan, who played most of the final three games with a broken thumb.

While the score was close deep into the third, the Canadians were decisively better and more energetic than the U.S. on the day as they took advantage of a draw that allowed them to play weak Belarus in the semifinal while the Americans had to battle to survive against Russia.

"They played very aggressively," Chelios said. "They had the confidence to do it and they did it. They played their game the whole game."

Following the disappointment of a fourth-place finish in the 1998 Winter Olympics at Nagano, Japan, the first Olympic hockey competition that included full participation of NHL players, this tournament comes as a shot in the arm to a nation working to improve its hockey development system.

Yesterday's final featured all of the positive elements of Canadian hockey, excellent goaltending, high emotion, intense physical play and skilful offensive movement, without the negative elements that have plagued Canada in international competition from time to time.

More important, three key players that weren't there for Canada when it mattered most in Nagano, Joe Sakic, Lemieux and winger Paul Kariya, all were major parts of the attack that saw Canada score 12 goals in its final two games.

The absence of the country's top goaltender, Patrick Roy, who declined to play for his country after suiting up in Nagano, turned out to be a negative that Team Canada was able to overcome.

Maple Leafs GM and head coach Pat Quinn guided this group of Canadians and said later that the Olympics have superseded NHL competition in his mind.

"As a young man growing up, the focus for me was not international hockey," said Quinn, who made the tough decision to bench his own goaltender, Curtis Joseph, after a tournament-opening loss to Sweden. "For me, the real hockey was the NHL. It wasn't until the influx of European players to the NHL that it began to change.

"The Olympics then took on a magnitude even bigger than the NHL, really."

Yesterday's game was expected to set TV records for hockey on both sides of the border and might boost the chances of the NHL continuing to participate in the Olympics. No decision has been made for the next Olympics in Italy four years down the road and the NHL and its players' association have both a World Cup planned for 2004 and a potentially destructive set of collective bargaining negotiations before it can commit to be part of Torino 2006.

"I hope the best players go again in '06," Gretzky said.

The Great One, however, was not willing to contemplate whether he would be willing to be in charge again.

"It's a long time away," he said. "Wanting to and doing it are two different things."

Eighteen of the 23 players on the Canadian roster now pursue their careers south of the border and will return to those teams today, but the impact of the moment yesterday seemed to pull them back to their Canadian roots.

"I grew up in Canada and played my minor hockey there until I was 18. Once you're born there, you're always a Canadian," Lemieux said. "You do whatever you can for your country."

NEILSON GAVE ALL TO GAME HE LOVES

CAM COLE

November 5, 2002 — *National Post*

HIS SENSE OF humour is so dry, and his facial expression so permanently worried, it takes a while after delivery to realize that Roger Neilson has just cracked a joke.

So it was, yesterday, when someone asked the newest inductee into the Hockey Hall of Fame builders' section how much preparation he had put into his acceptance speech.

"Oh, it's only four minutes long, so there's not much you can say there," he said, in the quiet gravelly voice of a man who's never been much good at clearing his throat. "Just thank a few people, and cut up the Leafs, and that's about it."

He is 68 years old now, the curly-haired innovator who has not only survived two types of cancer — or three, counting Harold Ballard — but a record eight head coaching jobs, subordinate positions with four other NHL teams, over 25 hockey seasons, and left behind a trail of devoted admirers at every stop along the way.

When the Hall's four new members — Neilson last, after St. Louis scoring whiz Bernie Federko, menacing winger Clark Gillies of the Islanders' dynasty and the Washington Capitals' classic stay-at-home defenceman, Rod Langway — were introduced at Air Canada Centre on Saturday night,

126

the ovation for Neilson was the kind that makes neck hair stand on end.

On and on it went, as Neilson, making bashful eye contact with the legends who lined the carpet applauding him, choked back tears that would have taken far too long to explain. Then, just before the ceremonial faceoff, he and fellow cancer survivor Saku Koivu, the Montreal Canadiens captain, shook hands, and an unmistakable look of shared triumph, and support, and hope, passed between them.

That was a moment so real, it could never have been staged.

"When I was out there on the ice, I kind of wondered what I was doing out there and whether I deserved all these honours," Neilson said yesterday. "But I think people realize, just like they did with Saku, that you're fighting a battle and they want to show they're on your side. I think it's nice that people feel that way."

If Neilson was the darling of the inductions last night, it's only natural. A Toronto boy whose first NHL coaching job was with the Maple Leafs, he probably has never done a more remarkable thing than in his very first season.

Asked if he found it ironic that he and Gillies, who played a prominent role in the Islanders' four-straight dismantling of Neilson's Vancouver Canucks in the 1982 Stanley Cup final, were going into the Hall together, Neilson rocked back on his heels and almost smiled.

"Well, the first time was with the '78 Leafs, and of course, we shut that line down, big-time," Neilson said, glancing across at the media scrum next door to see if Gillies had felt the needle.

In that seven-game upset, the rookie bench boss assigned a line of Jimmy Jones, Jerry Butler and Pat Boutette to check one of the greatest lines in NHL history — Bryan Trottier, Mike Bossy and Gillies — and the Leafs' trio ended the series plus-1. Unimaginable.

Of course, by then, Neilson had already made a name for himself as an innovator so clever, some hockey rules had to be changed to thwart his machinations. As a pro coach, he would be the first to make extensive use of video tape to analyze patterns in an opposing team's play, and among the first to use a form of the neutral-zone trap. For the former, he was dubbed Captain Video.

"It felt kinda dumb then, and it feels kinda dumb now, to be honest with you," said Neilson.

For the latter, he was cited as part of the problem in modern hockey, which its critics say is badly overcoached.

"If you're a coach, your job is to get your team to score goals and to stop the other team from scoring," said Neilson. "You want to be airtight defensively, and it's the other team's job to try to break through that, and that's how the game has always been played. There's always going to be coaches who come up with ways to stop a power play, stop a rush, and the offence has to figure out a way to break through it. That is sport."

Over the years, Neilson gained a reputation for scrupulous preparation, but also for absent-mindedness, so that a whole body of stories, some no doubt apocryphal, have clung to him. Like the time he called his neighbour, Tiger Williams, from Hawaii and said: 'Will you run over to my house and look on my front steps to see if my luggage is there?"

Or the time he walked into an Ottawa appliance store looking for a new video monitor and stopped a salesperson to ask: "Don't you have any TVs with a bigger screen than this?"

"Yes, sir, we do," said the salesman. "This is a microwave oven."

He bicycled to work in Florida, which he called his most enjoyable job, he hiked the mountains around Vancouver, he loved St. Louis and Buffalo, he might have had a Stanley Cup team in New York in 1993 if not for the strike, and he even enjoyed Philadelphia, though it ended badly for him there after his first cancer treatment, when GM Bobby Clarke famously said that Neilson "went goofy on us."

"It's just things that happen in pro sports," Neilson shrugged. "Bobby Clarke and I got along as well as any coach and GM could get along, both in Florida and Philadelphia. At the end, we had a major disagreement. I thought I was ready to coach, they didn't think I should. That's the way it is. Too bad it ended that way, but Bobby and I are still good friends."

No one has been able to stay mad at Neilson for very long, even in the wake of a heated playoff series. He's just too decent a human being. A mark of the regard in which he is held was when Ottawa head coach Jacques Martin, who hired Neilson as an assistant after the Flyers fiasco, stepped aside for one night in the 2000-01 season so that Neilson could coach his 1,000th game.

It was at a time when Neilson was determined to keep busy, keep active, and keep the cancer — myeloma, and malignant melanoma — at bay.

"I'm feeling pretty good, really," he said yesterday. "They change the medications around. There's two different cancers, and you have to kind of worry about both of them. Right now, the doctors are pretty happy. The great thing about medical science is, they've got all kinds of things to switch to. I could live forever, the way things are going."

He'd be a popular immortal.

As he walked carefully to centre ice Saturday, toward the Ken Danby painting commissioned by *Hockey Night in Canada*, Neilson — who claims no known relatives, has no grandchildren to play with and therefore no compelling reason to retire — saw two legends that almost stopped him in his tracks: the regal Jean Béliveau, and former Leafs captain Ted Kennedy.

"Growing up in North Toronto, Teeder was the Leafs' captain, and my favourite player," said Neilson. "I remember meeting him one day in a grocery store and he signed my hat. He was really my idol."

This time he did grin.

"Even at eight years old, I liked the checkers."

Last night, as he made his way among thousands of pairs of hands wanting to shake his, Neilson marvelled at the reception he always gets in Toronto, where he was once asked by Ballard to wear a paper bag over his head onto the bench as a gag, after Ballard had fired him and then, unable to find a replacement, rehired him.

"I don't know why people are so nice to me here," he said. "I guess, because of the Ballard thing, they sort of feel sorry for me.

"To me, this is the place for hockey. Here's the perfect example: When I was five years old, my family actually lived out on the island, Ward's Island, and I was just looking out my hotel window yesterday at the boat coming in. The Ward's boat is the one boat where they put some vehicles on it, but this time the deck was empty, and there were six kids playing ball hockey on the deck, pylons set up for nets, and they were having a great game all the way across the harbour.

"To me, that's Toronto, and that's Canada. It's hockey, and I wish Ken Danby had seen it. He'd have made a great painting of that."

(Ed. Note — Seven months after this story appeared, Roger Neilson lost his fight to cancer.)

RANGERS PASSED ON HOWE

BOB DUFF

September 23, 2003 — *The Windsor Star*

DETROIT — As the New York Rangers and Detroit Red Wings skated through pre-game warmups on the ice surface below, Gordie Howe stared down from his perch in the Joe Louis Arena press box and wondered how the axis of the hockey world might have been altered were fate to have kept him on his original path towards the National Hockey League.

In 1943, Howe, 15, attended his first NHL training camp, in Winnipeg with the Rangers.

"I was there four days," Howe recalled prior to Saturday's Rangers-Red Wings pre-season game, during which he discussed everything from his beginnings in hockey to his wife Colleen's battle with Pick's disease — and naturally, his legendary elbows. And about what course his life might have taken were the Rangers wise enough to get his name on a contract.

Howe was a youngster during the Depression, when money was scarce. Growing up, catalogues replaced shin pads as hockey equipment.

"My first day in camp with the Rangers, I watched the guy beside me get dressed, to see where everything went," Howe said.

Another hockey legend, Lester Patrick, who was the Gordie Howe of his era, coming out of retirement to play goal during the 1928 Stanley Cup final, ran the Rangers when the young Howe showed up amidst dozens of other prospects.

"He spoke to me four times," Howe said. "At the start of camp, he asked, 'What's your name, son?' and then they wrote it on a piece of paper and pinned it to the back of my sweater.

"The first day, I hit (Rangers veteran) Grant Warwick with a pretty good bodycheck and Mr. Patrick called me over and asked, 'What's your name, son?' Two other times, when I did something on the ice, he called me over and asked 'What's your name, son?' Finally, I said, 'It's on the back of my shirt, sir.'"

Unsigned, Howe went home to Saskatoon and the following fall, was invited to the Wings' training camp in Windsor.

He would score 786 goals during a 25-season NHL career.

He was assigned to Detroit's OHA junior club in Galt, but wasn't allowed to play because the Saskatchewan association wouldn't permit him a transfer. He practised all season with the team and participated in exhibition contests, learning the game from Al Murray, an NHL defenceman with the New York Americans.

"He came to me and said, 'I've got some news for you and you're not going to like it,'" Howe remembered. "That's when he told me my transfer didn't come through. But he told me if I stayed the year in Guelph, he'd make me into a hockey player, and he did."

Howe turned pro in 1945, playing for coach Tommy Ivan with Omaha of the U.S. League. The next spring, Ivan was promoted to Indianapolis of the AHL. Before training camp that fall, Detroit coach-GM Jack Adams told Ivan that Howe would be joining him at Indianapolis. "No," Ivan said. "He'll be playing for you."

He was right. Howe never saw the minor leagues again, skating in 1,787 NHL games and coming out of retirement in 1973 to play alongside sons Mark and Marty in the WHA, and for Canada during the 1974 Summit Series against the Soviet Union.

The nicest, most polite man you'd ever meet away from the rink, Howe was a ruthless assassin between the boards, especially when someone dared mess with a teammate, or worst of all, one of his kids.

"I remember a Russian player slashed Mark in the ear and cut him open," Howe recalled. "The next shift when we were out together, I had the puck and he was coming for me.

"I said, 'Oh, you want the puck? Well, here it is.' I threw it in the corner and when he went to get it, I broke his arm. After the game, he had to shake hands like this." Howe reached across his body and extended his left hand, still smiling devilishly at the memory.

Another Howe recollection involved his first time playing alongside Wayne Gretzky, with the WHA All-Stars against a Russian select squad. "There was a Russian hacking away at Wayne all night and he was getting really frustrated," Howe said. "I told him, 'The next time you get the puck, bring it up right wing. When you hear heavy breathing, get out of the way.'"

Howe leveled the Russian with a devastating check. As the Russian trainer tended to his prone player, the WHA team changed lines.

"We were sitting on the bench and I said, 'Damn,'" Howe remembered.

"Wayne asked, 'What's wrong, Gord?'"

"I said, 'He's getting up.'"

Howe doesn't make many public appearances these days, spending his days at his wife's side as Colleen Howe battles Pick's Disease, an illness similar to Alzheimer's disease in that it slowly steals a person's mind. Friends and family pitch in to help and allow Howe, 75, the chance to get out. Such as going to a Wings game.

"My dad can't sit in the seats, because he gets mobbed non-stop for autographs," Mark Howe said. "It's not that he doesn't appreciate the attention, but he feels badly for the people sitting around him, who never get to see the game."

More than 32 years after he wore his Red Wings sweater for the final time, the man they call Mr. Hockey is still Mr. Red Wing.

Detroit fans can only shudder at the thought of how easily Howe's star could have shone on Broadway.

ORR'S LEFT KNEE GONE FOR GOOD

DAMIEN COX

April 16, 2004 — *The Toronto Star*

BOSTON — Bobby Orr pressed his finger along the ridges of the long, red, ragged incision, hopeful that the daily throbbing pain of more than 30 years will soon be only a memory.

"I just got sick of being sick and sore," he said quietly.

The left knee that betrayed us all, Canada's most famous knee, has finally been retired for good, the frail and untrustworthy pieces of bone and cartilage removed to make room for a combination of chrome cobalt, titanium and polyethylene.

It won't give back to Orr — or to us — the joyous hockey moments he missed when he was forced to retire at age 30. Happily, that wasn't his dream when he underwent total knee replacement surgery Monday morning.

"I just hope I can go for a long walk," he said yesterday, smiling at his wife of 30 years, Peggy.

"It would be nice if we could ride bicycles," she suggested.

Three days after the complicated surgery, a procedure made more complex by the disastrous state of the patient's knee, Orr was weary but upbeat as he sat in his spacious hospital room on the 22nd floor of one of Boston's finest hospitals and gave his first post-surgery interview.

A flourish of floral arrangements and fruit baskets sat in various corners, a collection depleted by the removal of a few to Orr's downtown apartment when the jungle became too thick. An enormous arrangement sat on a nearby table, a riotous collection of purple and pink and green, courtesy of Orr's biggest fan, Donald S. Cherry.

"The biggest and the first," Orr said with a broad smile.

Barefoot, wearing a grey Reebok T-shirt and gray shorts, Orr held an ice bag against the newly repaired knee, with four separate large, white bandages covering the incision that stretched from six inches above his kneecap to halfway down his shin.

"I just want to be able to get up from a table and not have to push myself up," he said. "I don't need to play tennis or skate. I just would like to be a little more comfortable."

Sensing the moment was becoming too maudlin, Orr quickly brightened.

"Actually, my friends are afraid of me already," he chirped. "They're worried this is going to improve my golf swing."

For most of us who witnessed the exploits of the greatest hockey player who ever lived, he has never aged, or at least he has aged with remarkable restraint. Over the past decade, he has once again become more prominent in the game of his youth, appeared more frequently in the public eye and made thousands of individual days better because he made people feel like a friend.

It is almost always accompanied by that unmistakable Orr grin, the mischievous smile that would have followed a successful puck-between-the-legs move. A hairline that gently grayed but refused to recede made him, to those who wished it to be that way, forever young.

Yet Orr turned 56 on March 20 and for years he has laboured in constant pain, suffering quietly through a daily torment that friends understood. The cartilage in his knee, the tire tread, so to speak, was essentially gone and bone growths created by the absence of that cushion had deformed the knee, causing it to swell. Settling into an airplane seat was a painful experience.

Sixteen surgical explorations had left many scars but produced little comfort. The roar of the crowd had long been silenced, yet Orr continued to pay and pay and pay for doing what he had no choice but to do, taking the sublime talents he first imagined on the frozen Seguin River in Parry Sound and forging them into a comet-like professional career.

He arrived in the lineup of the Boston Bruins in the mid-'60s and changed the game. His Stanley Cup-winning goal in 1970 produced one of the most memorable sporting pictures ever, the image of a young Orr in flight.

"Every time I see Glenn Hall, he says the same thing," Orr said with a laugh, remembering his goaltending victim that day. "He always says, 'Was that the only goal you ever scored?'"

By 1976, Orr had amassed a pharaoh's stash of athletic gold and silver, but he was finished, other than six futile final matches in the fall of 1978 as a Chicago Blackhawk. There were other post-career disappointments, and it's a curious footnote that his two boys, Darren and Brent, never learned to skate, let alone play hockey.

"Hockey is a tough game, and the way I played, the way I wanted to play, meant I was hit and hit a lot," Orr said. "I was reckless. But if I had to do it again, I'd play the same way today, if I was allowed to. People talk about pressure and, in the end, when I started to feel the pressure was when I couldn't do any more what I once could."

He got over the sadness, eventually, but not the physical cost of trying to play on a knee first damaged in the 1966-67 season when he was hit by Maple Leafs defenceman Marcel Pronovost in a game at the Boston Garden.

"I still remember it. I was just trying to slip past him," said Orr, twisting in his seat to demonstrate as the memory flared. "My leg dragged behind me and he pinned it to the boards. That was it."

Post-retirement, the problems with the knee didn't go away, but became a silent enemy that would suddenly surprise with a sneak attack.

"Sure, I feel really bad for him. I felt really bad for a long time," Peggy said. "We'd be out walking or playing golf and then — boom! — the leg would give out on him."

But he didn't want this radical knee surgery. Quite frankly, it scared the hell out of him and there were the demands of his successful new career as an influential hockey agent that kept him on the move.

But so much of life had become a misery and then his back had started acting up because he had been compensating for the near uselessness of the left knee. Last April, he had surgery on the right knee, again related to the unwillingness of the confounded left one to contribute to basic, everyday living.

"Scotty Bowman called me," Orr said. "He said, 'Don't wait. I waited too long. Do it now.'"

John Davidson called, telling him the same thing. So, finally, he relented, met with Dr. Dennis Burke, an orthopedic surgeon who specializes in hip and knee replacement, and made plans to have the interior of the troublesome joint renovated.

"His knee was extremely bad," Burke said. "On a scale of 1 to 10, with 10 the worst, his was an 8 or a 9. He had completely lost all the cartilage."

While the concept of a total knee replacement conjures up images of the installation of a giant new hinge, the procedure is actually a "resurfacing" of the interface between the femur and tibia, adding new layers of alloy and plastic to allow the joint to operate more smoothly.

In Orr's case, his surgery was complicated by the multiple surgical scars on his knee and the fact he only had about a 70-degree arc of motion, about half that of a normal knee.

A plastic surgeon was consulted on skin care and ultimately Burke combined three of the old scars to create a new incision. A special technique that involved cutting into the shinbone was also needed because Orr's knee was so stiff. The result was an operation that lasted more than two hours, double what is normal.

It will take several months before Orr realizes the full benefits but, yesterday, despite a lack of sleep, nausea from pain medication and not having showered for four days, he was buoyant.

"I can't believe it," he said. "Before, with the other surgeries, it was always really sore afterwards. But unless there's something coming I'm not aware of, this is wonderful."

"I can't believe how much you can bend it already," Peggy said.

Good wishes have poured in, along with all the flowers. Former teammate Johnny Bucyk was due yesterday afternoon, while ex-Bruin Derek Sanderson was in on Wednesday.

"Sanderson was so funny," Orr said. "He was telling the nurses what medication they should be giving me."

The entry of a physiotherapist meant it was time for Orr to resume the process of rehabilitation, already in its second day, and with a handshake and a smile he professed his thanks to a visitor, gracious to a fault.

It was a mean trick, really, giving the guy all that talent, but also a knee of mush that meant he could only burn brightly for a short time.

Now, he'll settle for a pain-free stroll on a warm summer day. It all only means that we're growing old, too.

THE BEST CANADIAN JUNIORS EVER: CANADA 6, RUSSIA 1

ED WILLES

January 5, 2005 — *The Province (Vancouver)*

GRAND FORKS — Their moment is frozen in time. Literally.

Tuesday night, in the deep freeze which has become North Dakota, Team Canada's juniors ended seven years of frustration and performed that most underrated of sporting feats when they not only met the extraordinary expectations placed on them, but exceeded them.

The junior nats, who came into the 2005 World Junior Championships heralded as the most talented team Canada has ever sent to the tournament, fulfilled their destiny on Tuesday night when they crushed Russia 6-1 in front of a frenzied, sell-out crowd of 11,862, 11,860 of whom wore the tribal colours of The Maple Leaf. In winning the country's first gold since '97, the young Canadians finished the tournament with a perfect 6-0 record, outscored their opposition 41-7 and made the clear and unequivocal statement that they are the best team in tournament history.

"It's just the group of guys we had," said Winnipeg's Nigel Dawes, asked what he'll take out of this tournament. "I'll never forget the guys we had on this team. We went to war and nothing is better than beating the Russians.

"It's just such a great feeling. You're never, ever going to forget this. You're going to have these memories forever."

With the win over their archrivals, their first in four gold-medal showdowns with the Russians over the last six years, the Canadians became the seventh team to finish the tournament undefeated and untied since the World Junior Championships modern history began in '82. To be sure, there were great teams among that group, including the '95 Canadian gold-medal entry. But no team dominated the event in the manner The Leaf cruised through the tournament field. And no team put an exclamation mark on a perfect record the way the Canadians did on Tuesday night.

It started when Regina's Ryan Getzlaf scored 51 seconds after the opening faceoff and ended with a beery rendition of *O Canada* at the final horn. In between, Team Canada pounded the powerful Russians like a nail, driving starting goalie Anton Khudobin out of the game three minutes into the second period, holding stars Alexander Ovechkin and Evgeny Malkin off the scoresheet, and receiving six goals from six different players.

The victory, in fact, embodied the best parts of the Canadian game. It was artistic, as when Dawes found Anthony Stewart on the lip of the crease. It was violent, as when all-world defenceman Dion Phaneuf took out two Russians in the open ice, setting up tournament MVP Patrice Bergeron's goal. It was ugly, as when Jeff Carter drifted a wrister through the luckless Khodubin to start a four-goal, second-period run.

But mostly it was complete and almost ruthless in its execution.

"These guys are unreal," said Carter, who became Canada's all-time goal scorer in the tournament. "They're so talented. We could make plays but we could crash and bang, too."

"What can I say?" said Brent Sutter, the chief engineer of this machine. "It was a great effort by these young men but it's been the same since we first came together as a team."

Well, it's different now that they've delivered the gold but, as Sutter suggests, the most impressive thing about his group was their commitment to the cause. For three weeks their focus was almost frightening in its intensity. For three weeks, this salient was burned into their conscience.

Now, they have the ultimate prize and a place in the game's history. Suddenly three weeks of sacrifice seemed like a small price to pay for that reward.

"I was obviously nervous before the game but I also had a tremendous amount of confidence in this group," said Sutter. "We could see it the way they handled themselves every day. You could see these kids were professionals every step of the way."

And now they have something to share for the rest of their lives.

"It's a special group," said Andrew Ladd of Maple Ridge, B.C. "Obviously there's talent but it was more than that."

That much is obvious to the coaches, the 22 players — and 30 million of their closest friends.

Canada eats up Ovechkin

GRAND FORKS — Before the gold-medal game at the World Junior Championship, Alexander Ovechkin stopped in front of a television, heard his name mentioned and asked a Canadian media-type what the talking heads were discussing.

"They're saying Bergeron's line is going to play head-up against your line with Phaneuf and Weber on defence," Ovechkin was told.

"Good luck," he sneered.

As things turned out, luck was the last thing the Canadians needed against the Russian star.

Tuesday night, Russia's captain and emotional linchpin was taken out of the game, literally and figuratively, by a Canadian team who'd targeted him from the opening faceoff. In the first period, Ovechkin was hit cleanly and severely by, in succession, Sidney Crosby, Dion Phaneuf, Mike Richards and Patrice Bergeron. After Bergeron's hit late in the opening frame, Ovechkin came out for one shift in the second period, then called it a night.

He appeared on the interview podium after the game with his right arm in a sling.

"There was no point risking further injury," Russian coach Sergei Gersonsky said through an interpreter. "He's probably going to need surgery."

"Canada got the lead early, then they started to take the body," Ovechkin said through the same interpreter. "After that we couldn't come back."

Uncharacteristically, that was an understatement for Ovechkin.

With Canada holding both Ovechkin and Evgeny Malkin off the scoresheet, Russia's potent offence dried up against the Canadians' remorseless defence. The Russians produced just 11 shots on Canadian goalie Jeff Glass through the first two periods.

Glass, who was also called into question by Ovechkin after Sunday's semi-finals, enjoyed the last word in their private exchange. The Canadian goalie made three sharp saves during a 72-second five-on-three early in the first period when Canada was holding a 1-0 lead. Team Canada head coach Brent Sutter said those saves were a key moment in the game.

"I wasn't going to get into a battle of words," Glass said. "I was going to let my play do the talking for me. We have gold medals around our necks right now, and he's left with nothing. Sometimes when you say something like that it can bite you in the rear."

"We weren't trying to knock (Ovechkin) out of the game," Phaneuf said. "But he's a top player and you have to take the body against him."

Which was a popular theme for Team Canada.

"They're a talented team," said Andrew Ladd. "We wanted them to pay a price every time they touched the puck."

PERMISSIONS

The following were reprinted with permission from the *National Post* where they were originally published on the dates stated below.

Blatchford, Christie, "Mercurys Pass the Great Torch," February 25, 2002

Cole, Cam, "The Kid, the Karma and Time," April 17, 1999

MacGregor, Roy, "How Rome was Built in Seven Painful Years," January 25, 1999

Blatchford, Christie, "Rocket Always Master of His House," May 31, 2000

MacGregor, Roy, "The Lion in Winter," March 24, 2001

Cole, Cam, "Neilson Gave All to Game He Loves," November 5, 2002

The following were reprinted with permission from *Montreal Gazette* where they were originally published on the dates stated below.

Fisher, Red, "Lighting the Flame of Revolution," September 26, 2004

Fisher, Red, "The Man in the Mask," September 24, 2004

Fisher, Red, "New Year's Eve Bash," September 23, 2004

Strachan, Al, "Cherry Loses With Class," May 11, 1979

Farber, Michael, "Jones Takes On Career Challenge," August 10, 1988

Fisher, Red, "What Really Counts: A Visit with Toe Blake," December 18, 1991

Farber, Michael, "McSorley's Stick Call Recalls Cherry's Blunder," June 4, 1993
Farber, Michael, "Roy Reigns as Best Player of the Second Season," June 8, 1993

The following were reprinted with permission from the *Vancouver Sun* where they were originally published on the dates stated below.
Taylor, Jim, "Benny and the Jet," June 28, 1972
Taylor, Jim, "Henderson's Supernatural Trick," September 29, 1972
McMartin, Pete, "What a Thriller: Team Canada Captures Fabulous Series On Gretzky-to-Lemieux Winning Goal," September 16, 1987

The following were reprinted with permission Torstar Syndication Services, by which they were they were originally published on the dates stated below.
Dunnell, Milt, "Best Shot Came from A Needle," April 24, 1964
Cox, Damien, "Gold Rush, Eh? Hockey Victory Crowning Achievement Of Olympic Effort," February 25, 2002
Cox, Damien, "Orr's left Knee Gone For Good," April 16, 2004

The following were reprinted with permission from the *Globe and Mail* where they were originally published on the dates stated below.
Beddoes, Dick, "The Word is Defiance," May 3, 1967
Maki, Allan, "Golden Redemption for Canada's Women," February 22, 2002

The following was reprinted with permission from Sun Media. The story originally was published in the *Calgary Sun* on the date stated below.
Taylor, Jim, "The Great Ones," April 19, 1999

The following was reprinted with permission from Southam News Syndication Services.
Coleman, Jim, "Never a Doubt," September 29, 1972
Coleman, Jim, "The Soviets Can't Beat Our Best." January 12, 1976

The following were reprinted with permission from *Edmonton Journal* where they were originally published on the dates stated below.
Matheson, Jim, "Skalbania Signs Young Gretzky," June 12, 1978
Jones, Terry, "The Greatest!" December 31, 1981
Matheson, Jim, "Unbelievable," December 31, 1981
Matheson, Jim, "Oilers Quench An Old Thirst," May 20, 1984
Cole, Cam, "Ancient Edifice Pulls the Plug," May 25, 1988
Cole, Cam, "The Greatest Trade or The Great Charade?" August 10, 1988

The following were reprinted with permission from the *Calgary Herald* where they were originally published on the dates stated below.

Maki, Allan, "Champs Gave All They Had," May 26, 1989

Duhatschek, Eric, "Former Flames' Coach Succumbs to Brain Tumour," November 27, 1991

The following were reprinted with permission from *The Province* (Vancouver) where they were originally published on the dates stated below.

Taylor, Jim, "New Miracle on Ice," May 1, 1994

Willes, Ed, "The Best Canadian Juniors Ever: Canada 6, Russia 1," January 5, 2005

Willes, Ed, "Canada Eats Up Ovechkin," January 5, 2005

The following were reprinted with permission from *Ottawa Citizen* where they were originally published on the dates stated below.

Kinsella, Jack, "Long Live the King And Leafs the Name," April 23, 1962

MacGregor, Roy, "Great End to a Year to Forget," January 3, 1995

MacGregor, Roy, "Ms. Hockey: If Gretzky was a Woman his Name Would Be Wickenheiser," March 22, 1997

Scanlan, Wayne, "No Regrets: The Canadian Hockey Team Boss Says He Spoke Out, Loudly, To 'Protect' His Players," February 20, 2002

The following was reprinted with permission from *Windsor Star* where it was originally published on the date stated below.

Duff, Bob, "Rangers Passed on Howe," September 23, 2003